Diamonds and Death
The True, Tragic Tale of
Diamond Bessie Moore

ENJOY THE STORY
OF DIAMOND BESSIE!

[signature]

Mitchel Whitington

ISBN 978-1-9393061-1-1

First Edition

Printed in the United States of America
Published by 23 House Publishing
SAN 299-8084
www.23house.com

A Dedication

At the writing of this book, the *Diamond Bessie Murder Trial*[©] play has been performed for over sixty consecutive years. It is not only a tradition, but has in itself become a part of Jefferson's history. There have been many people associated with the play over time, but there are two in particular who have carried the torch of Diamond Bessie over the years and deserve a special recognition.

Milton Jones was in the play from the second-ever performance until he retired from it just a few years ago, having played the part of Jim, Sam the Gravedigger, the Coroner, the Janitor and finally the Judge. It wasn't that long ago that the actor portraying the Gravedigger couldn't make a performance, and Milton was quickly drafted to step into the role once again, which he did without hesitation.

Margaret Jones has been involved in the wardrobe, makeup, and production of the play for many years, and she was the director from 1996 to 2008. Even after she retired from the position, Margaret is often there backstage, ready to help out in any possible capacity.

Because of their love of the *Diamond Bessie Murder Trial*[©] play, their immeasurable contribution to it, and their continued dedication to the production, this book is lovingly and respectfully dedicated to…

Milton and Margaret Jones

May the future productions of the play over the years to come honor you by continuing the high standards that you have set for it throughout your lives.

Table of Contents

Foreword by the Author

The first spark to become a writer came for me in 1978; in the years since, I have become an avid student of history and love immersing myself in the projects that I undertake. In all those years of research and writing, I must confess that I've never come across a topic with as much interesting, yet conflicting information as the murder of Diamond Bessie. The misinformation is simply staggering.

For example, I found published reports that Bessie's body was discovered by a young lady, by a man visiting Jefferson from New Orleans, and even by a group of freed slaves.

As to the topic of Diamond Bessie's marital status, several sources report the marriage occurred in Linden, Texas; others that it was in Danville, Illinois; additional news articles indicate only a common law marriage; and some hold the

1

stance that no marriage existed between her and Abe Rothschild at all.

In this book, I have attempted to uncover the truth, in many cases looking back to the actual records from the trials held after Bessie's murder. I have also quoted newspaper articles from the day to provide information to the reader exactly as it was given to the public as the story was unfolding. Writing this book has been a challenge, but also an extremely enjoyable endeavor – like trying to solve a Rubik's Cube of information from over a century ago.

The sheer magnitude of information that I found proved to be almost unbelievable. Between the court records, the newspaper articles from the period, and the published information that has been written over the decades since, a complete and unabridged account of the murder and subsequent trials would span several volumes. These would definitely be tedious and completely unreadable.

I therefore set out to tell the story of Bessie and Abe in a complete manner, without getting too bogged down in the non-essential details. Some information has been omitted for the sake of brevity and readability – mostly aspects of the case that do not affect the story one way or another, are redundant, or do not have enough backing evidence to include.

Instead of focusing on every witness brought to the Habeas Corpus hearing and the two trials, I have endeavored to discuss only those with unique information, or that were pertinent to the case itself. As you can imagine with any legal case of this magnitude, there are a lot of peripheral things going on that would only bog down the story. For example, there is a police detective named Colonel Thomas E. Snelbaker who was accused by other parties of either blackmailing or extorting Abe Rothschild's father in conjunction with the trial, or lurking around Jefferson, his presence being kept secret so that he could serve as a surprise state's witness. His story is so convoluted and confusing that adding it would not enhance the story of Diamond Bessie and Abe Rothschild, and it is not material to the ultimate outcome. Such fringe stories have been omitted in order to tell a readable, yet still comprehensive story.

I believe that the account that I have provided is accurate, and I hope that you find it interesting. Even more so, I hope that you, the reader, enjoy this terrible story of diamonds and death... the true, tragic tale of Diamond Bessie Moore.

The author after a long day of sifting through court records
in the archive room of the Jefferson Historical Museum.

A Gruesome Discovery

On a cold, Wednesday afternoon, February 5, 1877, a woman named Sarah King was trudging through the snow south of Big Cypress Bayou in Jefferson looking for downed limbs that could be used for firewood to heat her home in the frigid winter weather. She suddenly made a very grisly discovery.

The dead body of a woman was lying on the ground, her back on a small mound, her head uphill, her left hand across her body, a hat obscuring the left side of her head and eye.[1]

The face, eyes and nose of the dead woman were covered with bugs.[2] Sarah later said, "I went within six or eight feet of

---

[1] Ex Parte Abe Rothschild, Court of Appeals of Texas, 2 Tex. Ct. App. 560; 1877 Tex. Crim. App. Lexis 188, p.2.

the body. I did not stay there at all. I left in a walk!"[3] Many have speculated that it was probably a fast walk indeed.

After crossing the bridge back to Jefferson, she encountered a man named Sims, and she told him what she had found. She asked him to relay the information to Judge Bickford, who was the Justice of the Peace and Coroner for Marion County.[4]

Sims did just that, and Justice Bickford quickly put together a group of men to serve as the Coroner's jury, and proceeded out into the woods to the location of the body.

The spot where the body was found was very secluded – between two roads, but visible from neither, and barely reached by direct sunshine for more than two hours on any given day.[5]

It appeared that the victim had been shot in the left temple, and from the burning of her hair in that area, it had clearly been delivered at a very close range. There appeared to be a slight swelling of the body, and the fingernails had turned purple.[6]

A.J. Stambaugh, a constable in Jefferson, was present at the scene and searched the area. About thirty feet from the body was a beer bottle that contained a small quantity of "some kind of liquid," a cork that looked like that of a pickle-bottle, and some ordinary brown wrapping-paper on which there were light-bread crumbs, chicken bones, and fragments of pickles[7] – all apparently remnants of a picnic.

Dr. J.G. Eason, who also accompanied the coroner to the scene, felt that the body had been carefully laid out, with the

---

[2] Ex Parte Abe Rothschild, Court of Appeals of Texas, 2 Tex. Ct. App. 560; 1877 Tex. Crim. App. Lexis 188, p. 2.

[3] Walters, Mahlon L. "Who Done It to Whom?" Texas Bar Journal, 1963, p. 2.

[4] Ibid.

[5] Op.cit., Ex Parte Abe Rothschild, p. 2.

[6] Ibid.

[7] Ibid.

woman's hat set to the left side of the head to cover the bullet wound. He found powder-burn around the wound and on the edge of the hat. The wound was just at the edge of the woman's hair, and it was infested with maggots.[8]

Probing the wound, he found that the bullet went downwards and back, not exiting the body but instead lodging in the bone of the right ear. He felt that the wound would have caused instant death in the victim. The body showed little sign of decomposition, except in and around the wound, and around the joints.[9]

Stambaugh, the constable, observed that the body "looked to him as natural as life," but on close examination he saw that the fingernails had turned purple, and the body was swollen around the bowels. Stanbraugh also said that he recognized the body as that of a lady that he had seen on the streets of Jefferson two weeks before. She was alone at the time, but he remembered noticing her because of the style of dress that she was wearing.[10]

Dr. Eason also recognized the woman, having seen her in Jefferson once on Saturday, January 20, and twice the next morning. Each time she was in the company of her husband, "A. Monroe."[11]

The woman's body was located "to the right of the road going to Marshall, just after you rise the hill down a slant from the road."[12] It was 1300 yards from the end of the bridge over

---

[8] Ex Parte Abe Rothschild, Court of Appeals of Texas, 2 Tex. Ct. App. 560; 1877 Tex. Crim. App. Lexis 188, p. 2.

[9] Ibid.

[10] Ibid.

[11] Ibid.

[12] Walters, Mahlon L. "Who Done It to Whom?" Texas Bar Journal, 1963, p. 2.

Big Cypress Bayou and 200 yards east of the public road leading to Marshall.[13]

After the examination and documentation of the crime scene, the body was removed to the coroner's office in town, where it remained that night and the next day and evening before interment in Jefferson's Oakwood Cemetery... and so began one of Texas' most intriguing, unsolved mysteries – the murder of Diamond Bessie.

---

[13] Op.cit., Ex Parte Abe Rothschild, p. 2.

The Lovers Meet

"Diamond Bessie" was born as Annie Stone, the daughter of a shoe merchant in Syracuse, New York in 1854. According to *The National Police Gazette*, she was raised, *"surrounded by all the advantages of a pleasant home, a fond mother, indulgent father, troops of friends and a polite education. She grew into girlhood, the idol of her father, the pet of a select circle. From girlhood and its bright dreams of innocence, she budded into young womanhood and her unusual personal beauty soon attracted a number of ardent and sincere admirers, all anxious to win so desirable a prize, and obtain possession of a jewel so rare. Of graceful form and well-proportioned figure, Miss Stone was among her young lady acquaintances.*

"Her features were rather after the Greek model; the well-chiseled lips that smiled in scorn, the graceful contour of bust, the long hair that floated down her alabaster shoulders in rich profusion; the brilliant eyes that now sparkled with mirth or drooped in sadness, made up the picture of one of the loveliest women of her time.

"She was the eldest sister, and early exhibited a tendency to literary pursuits, and had not the web of destiny been wound around its victim, she might have graced the literary world as she did the social circle. Among the many admirers of Miss Annie in Syracuse, there was one heartless, soulless young man, who on the most solemn promises ever breathed into maiden's ear, seduced and then deserted her, after keeping her as his mistress for some length of time."[14]

This seduction occurred when Annie was only fifteen years of age, by a gentleman only known by his surname of Moore. They were together for a short time, and upon their breakup she "took one more step downward toward the hell of woman's infamy" as the *National Police Gazette* reported, and became a public prostitute in Cincinnati, Ohio, where she became well known at the establishment of Miss Frank Wright's "Mansion of Joy" in that city.[15] One has to wonder how severely the breakup must have affected her, to transform her from a proper young woman to a notorious lady of the evening.

She became quite popular in Cincinnati in that occupation, and because of her love for diamonds, her wealthy clients often gave them to her as presents, and in consideration for the affection that she provided them.[16]

---

[14] "Diamond Bessie – Strange and Sad History of a Beautiful Young Girl," *The National Police Gazette*, May 21, 1878, p. 7.

[15] Ibid.

[16] Russell, Traylor. *The Diamond Bessie Murder and the Rothschid Trials* (Waco: Texian Press, 1971), p. 9.

Prostitutes tend to move from time to time to find new clients and to avoid prosecution from the authorities, and Annie Stone was no exception. She drifted from Cincinnati to New Orleans, Louisiana, and then up to Hot Springs, Arkansas, sometimes giving her name as Annie Moore, adopting the surname of her first love.[17]

She could have worked in any one – or more – of Hot Springs' brothels of the day: the Hatterie Hotel operated by Madam Grace Goldstein, the West End Hotel run by Josephine Belmont from New Orleans, or the Pigley Rooms whose madam was Evelyn Anderson.[18] It was no matter, though; regardless of which establishments held her employ at the time, her life would change forever when a man named Abe Rothschild walked through the door.

* * * * *

Abraham Rothschild was the son of Maier Rothschild, a wealthy jewel merchant, who lived at 264 W. Fifth Street in Cincinnati. He represented the Rothschild family as a traveling salesman, or "drummer" as they were known in that day.

Only twenty-three years of age, he was and is a man of firm physique and prepossessing appearance, but dissipated reckless and dissolute. On account of his dissipation he was, sometime before the murder, discharged from the employ of a New York notion house. The year before the murder he had been disowned by his parents.[19]

* * * * *

---

[17] Russell, Traylor. *The Diamond Bessie Murder and the Rothschid Trials* (Waco: Texian Press, 1971), p. 9.

[18] Raines, Robert K. *Hot Springs: Images of America* (Mount Pleasant, SC: Arcadia Pubishing, 2013), p. 10.

[19] Walters, Mahlon L. "Who Done It to Whom?" Texas Bar Journal, 1963, p. 6.

Both Annie/Bessie and Abe were known to use alcohol to access and quarrel to the point of violence. In December, 1875 the couple were in Cincinnati and were seen in public, drunk and fighting. Rothschild was beating his female companion on the street. A young man approached and asked that he stop hurting her, to which Abe pulled his pistol and pointed it at the lad. He then recognized the boy and didn't shoot; instead he dragged Bessie down the street, continuing to beat her. They soon arrived at Miss Frank Wright's "Mansion of Joy," a former place of employment for Bessie, and Rothschild rang for admittance. Miss Wright stuck her head out of a window and called, "You can't get in here! Go away!"[20]

When the Republican National Convention was held in Cincinnati in 1876, Abe apparently saw the business potential with all of the men coming to town.

The 1876 Republican National Convention in Cincinnati

---

[20] Russell, Traylor. *The Diamond Bessie Murder and the Rothschid Trials* (Waco: Texian Press, 1971), p. 18.

He demanded that Bessie work as a prostitute and bring him $50 every day – in today's world Rothschild would be known as a pimp for such a business arrangement. When she failed to meet that quota on one particular day, he beat her so violently that he was arrested.[21]

The Cincinnati *Enquirer* traced their travels with the following news story from 1878:

Where he first met her is not known, but she came to this city [Cincinnati] with him on a steamer from New Orleans in the spring of 1876, she pawning her baggage to the Captain on the arrival of the boat here for the fare of the two. She had some diamonds with her then, which she shortly deposited with Gilmore, Dunlap & Co. as collateral for a loan. She and Rothschild then went to a room on Seventh Street, and Rothschild afterward took her to Frank Wright's to board. He visited her there, and the pair used to quarrel frequently, Rothschild on several occasions beating her in a terrible manner, she claimed, in order to force her to give up her diamonds to him. Miss Wright told at the time that Rothschild used to whip Bessie because the wages of her shame were not larger, and would reproach her with the fact that other girls in the house made more money than she.[22]

After leaving the Wright mansion, Bessie went to one or two "houses" here, where she stayed a short time, and finally went to Chicago. She returned to this city and got her diamonds out of pawn, and then after paying another visit to Chicago, left that city on the 11th of January, 1877, accompanied by Rothschild. Before leaving Chicago, she told the landlady of the house where she stayed that Rothschild had offered to marry her, but the woman warned her that it was

[21] Russell, Traylor. *The Diamond Bessie Murder and the Rothschid Trials* (Waco: Texian Press, 1971), p. 18.
[22] "The Story of the Killing of Diamond Bessie," *The Cincinnati Daily Enquirer*, December 25, 1878, p. 2.

only her diamonds he wanted, and not to be fooled by him. When she left Chicago she had in her possession a solitaire diamond ring valued at $400, a cluster diamond ring valued at $600, a heavy gold locket and chain valued at $200, and a pair of gold bracelets with cameo setting, besides other articles of jewelry, valued in all at about $1,500. The pair started for Texas.[23]

---

[23] "The Story of the Killing of Diamond Bessie," *The Cincinnati Daily Enquirer,* December 25, 1878, p. 2.

A Question of Marriage

The question as to whether or not Bessie and Abe were married has puzzled historians for over a century – there is certainly a plethora of conflicting information.

There can be no question that when the couple arrived in Jefferson, Texas on January 18, 1877 and checked into the Brooks House Hotel, they registered in Room No. 4 as "A. Monroe and wife."[24]

But since the name itself was a lie, was the notation of "wife" untrue as well?

In the court case where Abe Rothschild was seeking bail pending trial after his arrest for the murder of Diamond Bessie, Jennie Simpson, chamber-maid at the Brooks House, testified that she had asked the lady accompanying "A. Monroe" how long they had been married. She made no reply, but the gentleman spoke up and said that they had been married two years. Jennie then asked why the lady did not tell her name. The lady said nothing, but "A. Monroe" said only that she was

[24] Walters, Mahlon L. "Who Done It to Whom?" Texas Bar Journal, 1963, p. 2.

his wife, and re-stated that they had been married for two years.[25]

Although there is no credible evidence that the couple had been married for two years, perhaps he was alluding to the time that they had simply been together.

In W.H. Ward's *History of Jefferson*, published in 1900, the author asserts that the couple was married in Linden, Texas, about eighteen miles north of Jefferson. The text says:

"The woman remained true and steadfast to the man she loved, for whom she had given up her innocence and her home. Through all this she had relied upon Rothchild's promise to make her his wife, and she prayed that the promise might be fulfilled.

"Finding her prayers of no avail, she demanded a fulfillment of the pledge. There was a scene, of course, and other scenes followed. Rothchild had now to deal, not with a sill trusting girl, but with a wronged, outraged and desperate woman, who battled not only for her rights, but for her child, yet unborn. In a fit of desperation she threatened to lay the shameful story of her betrayal before Rothchild's father, a wealthy and influential citizen of Cincinnati. Then Rothchild is alleged to have conceived and proceeded to carry out a crime so dark, so despicable, and so diabolical that Satan himself must have blushed at its conception. He promised the young girl to make her his wife. He told her that it would not do for them to be married in Cincinnati, where both themselves and their intimacy were so well known, but that he would take her on one of his western trips. Rothchild was a traveling salesman, representing a big jewelry house in which his father was financially interested, and he himself being slated for partnership, and that by changing one figure in the marriage

---

[25] Ex Parte Abe Rothschild, Court of Appeals of Texas, 2 Tex. Ct. App. 560; 1877 Tex. Crim. App. Lexis 188, p. 3.

certificate it would make it appear that they had been married immediately upon the young girl's leaving home, which would have given legitimate birth to the child to which Bessie Moore was about to become the mother.

"The girl believed him and blessed him, and they left Cincinnati together, traveling westward and passing through Texarkana. From the moment Rothchild promised to make Bessie Moore his wife he had been planning the woman's murder. They left the Texas & Pacific Railway at Kildare, Rothchild telling the woman that they would go through Linden, the county seat of Cass County, to be married, choosing that spot, he said, because it was so obscure that news of the marriage would not be heard outside of the little town in which the ceremony was to be performed. His real intention was to murder the woman on the road. He was thwarted in this by being compelled to make the trip on a public coach, there being no such things as private conveyances in Kildare.

"Once at Linden, Rothchild was compelled to make good his promise and Bessie Moore, the wronged and betrayed girl, became Bessie Rothchild, the wife of her betrayer. From Linden they came to Jefferson, Texas, from which point it was agreed that Mrs. Rothchild should return to Cincinnati and have her marriage certificate recorded, after which she was to return to her husband. The poor girl looked forward with eagerness and hunger to the day she should return to her home bearing the honored name of wife, and be clasped once more in her mother's arms. They reached Jefferson and registered at the Brooks Hotel."[26]

Searching the marriage records for Cass County, Texas, in the year range from 1847-2002 reveals no licenses issued to a

---

[26] "The Murder of Diamond Bessie," *Frontier Times*, Vol. 14, No 8, May 1937, p. 321.

Bessie Moore and Abe Rothschild, or even an Annie Stone and Abe. Also, most accounts show Abe and Bessie traveling to Marshall, Texas before Jefferson, not Linden.

Marriage is also noted in a story about Abe Rothschild from the Washington *Bee*. The June 24, 1899 edition says: *He [Rothschild] first came into public notice in 1877, when he married a woman known in the West as "Diamond Bessie" Moore, and induced her to go to Jefferson, Tex., where he registered at a hotel as "A. Monroe and wife."*

Another account has the couple marrying in Danville, Illinois, prior to their arrival in Jefferson. The text of the marriage license is as follows:

MARRIAGE LICENSE
To any person legally authorized to solemnize Marriage, Greeting.
Marriage may be celebrated

Between Abe Rothschilds of New Orleans
In the parish of Orleans and State of Louisiana
Of the age of 24 years and

Miss Bertha Moore of Chicago
In the County of Cook and State of Illinois
Of the age of 22 years.

Witness John W. Dale, County Clerk
And the seat of said county at his office in Danville in said County this 10th day of January, A.D. 1877

Although Rothschild's name is incorrectly spelled as "Rothschilds," and Bessie's name is erroneously listed as

"Bertha," it is clear that both used aliases throughout their lives. If this is their marriage license, then there is no reason to expect that it would be different in this case.

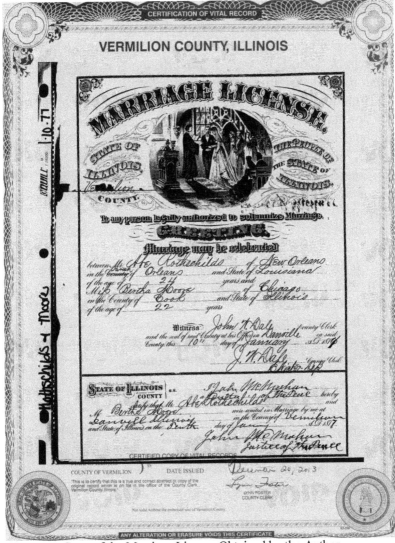

Copy of the Marriage License Obtained by the Author

19

The Danville marriage is further supported by a story in The National Police Gazette, page 7, May 21, 1878:

It is evident that, fallen as she was, the girl had conceived a sincere love for him, which the demon could neither appreciate nor return. About two weeks before the murder, Rothschild and the doomed woman left Cincinnati and together went to Danville, Ill., where they were married. Thence they came to Jefferson, Texas, she doubtless believing he intended to get a home there and take up residence.

Finally, Mahlon L. Walters wrote an article for the Texas Bar Journal in February, 1963, using as his resource the Files of the Marshall *News Messenger* newspaper, 1880. In his article, Walters noted:

About a fortnight before the murder, the pair left Cincinnati and went to Danville, Ind., where they were married.[27]

On Friday, July 27, 1877, The Cincinnati *Enquirer* published a letter to the editor:

Please let me know, through your valuable paper, in what town and state Abe Rothschild married Bessie Moore, and oblige a daily subscriber.

The editor replied in the paper:

We were not invited to the ceremony, but understand it was at Danville, Vermillion County, Illinois.[28]

* * * * *

Jefferson's newspaper *The Jimplecute* is the fifth-oldest newspaper in Texas, having been founded in 1848. When recounting the story of Diamond Bessie, two different reporters

---

[27] Walters, Mahlon L. "Who Done It to Whom?" Texas Bar Journal, 1963, p. 7.
[28] "A Happy Couple," The Cincinnati *Enquirer*, Cincinnati, Ohio, July 27, 1877, p. 8.

came to different conclusions concerning their marriage in stories published twenty-eight years apart. In a story titled "Diamond Bessie Is Marion County's Most Famous Murder Case," published on April 11, 1937, the reporter writes that the couple was married in Linden. Another story titled "Diamond Bessie Case One of Most Notorious in Texas History" published on June 17, 1965, the reporter recounts the Danville, Illinois version of the marriage story.

* * * * *

Perhaps the definitive word on the subject of their marriage can be found in the March 3, 1877 edition of the *Cincinnati Enquirer*, Cincinnati, Ohio:

Abe Rothschild's Marriage

The following from the Danville (Ills.) News, of January 11, 1876, may be accepted as conclusive evidence of the marriage of Abe Rothschild to Bessie Moore:

She was as pretty as a picture. Her auburn hair, French twist, contrasted handsomely with her large blue eyes. Her lovely complexion and graceful form would have fired the heart of an Italian sculptor. She was attired in traveling habit, and said she had embraced the freezy breezes of Chicago for eighteen years. Her name, if any one was so inquisitive as to ask, was Miss Bertha Moore.

He was an exile from Jerusalem, and supported the characteristic beak, under which a promising mustache had made its appearance. His curly ringlets were parted near the center, and one could almost see the perfumed waters sparkling over the lapels of his coat. He was from the Sunny South, and registered as Abe Rothschild, New Orleans.

They arrived, as by appointment, in the city yesterday afternoon, and drove to the Aetna House, where matters were arranged and the date, day and hour settled. All that was needed now was a dollar's worth of parchments with the County Clerk's autograph attached thereto, and some obliging person with authority in such cases. These were at hand, and before the hasty couple knew what a beautiful city they were in, and before they had strolled hand in hand through our parks, or visited our skating rink, or even viewed our much talked-of monument in the Public Square, they were married. Justice McMahan officiating, the nuptials were tied at the Atena House.

A reporter offered the congratulations of The News to the happy pair last night and found them in room 52, making preparations for a journey into the land of Morpheus, but they intended to change cars at 1:10 this morning and go south via E., T., H. and C. Bon voyage, Mr. and Mrs. A. Rothschild. [29]

The newspaper article uses several expressions from the day that can be lost in translation. For example, the colorful reference to Abe as "an exile from Jerusalem" was simply a way of saying that he was of the Jewish religion. The couple preparing for "a journey into the land of Morpheus" was a reference to the Morpheus, the Greek God of dreams, and was fanciful way of saying they were preparing for bed. The "E., T., H. and C." was a railroad servicing Danville, Illinois, and the one that the couple took to begin their ill-fated journey that would end in a murder in Jefferson. It is ironic that the reporter wished them "bon voyage," which after all, means "safe journey."

---

[29] "Abe Rothschild's Marriage," The Cincinnati *Enquirer*, March 3, 1877, p. 4.

The Couple Arrives in Jefferson

When the passenger train pulled into Jefferson on Friday, January 19, 1877, it was met with the usual fanfare. There was the traditional blowing of the whistle and the ringing of the train bell, the excitement of the crowd gathered to meet friends and relatives on the train, and the calls from the carriage drivers from Haywood House, Excelsior House, and Brooks House as they tried to gather business from new visitors to town.[30]

Dr. J.H. Turner was the landlord of the Brooks House hotel in 1877, and in testimony later given in court, he first saw a man and woman on that Friday at the Jefferson train station

[30] Russell, Traylor. *Carpetbaggers, Scalawags & Others*. Waco: Texian Press, 1973, p. 80.

who expressed interest in his establishment. He took them by horse-drawn cart to the Brooks House, where they registered as "A. Monroe and wife" for Room No. 4.[31] The couple had a trunk and a valise with them, and the trunk was marked, "A. Moore, N.O." on the leather below the handle on the side.[32]

H.J. Donovan, the baggage-master of the railroad at Jefferson, also saw "Monroe" and his wife disembarking, and personally removed their luggage from the train. He noticed the name "Annie Moore" on the top of the trunk.[33]

The Brook House on Vale Street in Jefferson

---

[31] Walters, Mahlon L. "Who Done It to Whom?" Texas Bar Journal, 1963, p. 2.

[32] Ex Parte Abe Rothschild, Court of Appeals of Texas, 2 Tex. Ct. App. 560; 1877 Tex. Crim. App. Lexis 188, p. 2.

[33] Ibid. p.3.

From the start, other people at the Brooks House heard quarrelling between "A. Monroe and wife" in their room. W.T. Armistead, who later served as one of Rothschild's attorneys, was staying there at the time. He later said that the couple was in the room next to him, and on Saturday evening he was kept awake all night by their loud arguing. A chambermaid, Jennie Simpson, heard them fighting that evening as well. Jennie Simpson entered the Monroe room a number of times in the course of the next day for her housekeeping chores, and at one point found Bessie weeping bitterly.[34]

One account of their stay at the Brooks House reports that there were sounds of slaps and heavy blows from behind the closed door of the room, and that a man's voice could be heard reading a newspaper, as if to drown out the sobbing of his wife.[35]

A trunk was delivered to the Brooks House from the train station and left on the front porch to be carried upstairs, and Dr. J.H. Turner noticed that near the handle were the words: "A. Moore, New Orleans."[36]

On Saturday, the couple was seen strolling all around town; her fine clothes and diamonds turned many heads. They became familiar figures in the few days that they were in Jefferson and were the talk of the town.[37]

They frequented the various saloons around town, likely including the most popular drinking establishment in Jefferson, The Rosebud.[38]

---

[34] Russell, Traylor. *The Diamond Bessie Murder and the Rothschild Trials.* Waco: Texian Press, 1971,

[35] Parmelee, Deolece. *The Deadly Jewels of Diamond Bessie.* Jefferson, Texas: The Jessie Allen Wise Garden Club. 1868. p. 2.

[36] Ibid., p. 3.

[37] Op.cit., Russell, p. 20.

[38] Ibid.

"A. Monroe" wore a long, brown chinchilla coat and a rollbrim hat as he strolled around town.[39]

Later in the day, "A. Monroe" was spotted going into the Ballauf & Company Hardware Store alone where he purchased a "pistol and cartridges," according to the Shreveport *Times*.[40]

R. Ballauf & Co. Hardware, Austin Street, Jefferson, Texas

On Sunday morning, Bessie seemed to have recovered her cheerfulness and gave Jennie the maid a handsome present, a piece of jewelry, telling her that she and her husband had not

[39] Parmelee, Deolece. *The Deadly Jewels of Diamond Bessie*. Jefferson, Texas: The Jessie Allen Wise Garden Club. 1868. p. 2.
[40] Woods, Larry J. "New Speculation about Murder of Diamond Bessie," Jefferson *Jimplecute*, December 11, 1997.

been very happy for some time past but that they were entirely reconciled and were going out in the woods to spend the day.[41]

The couple took their breakfast at the hotel the morning of Sunday, January 21, and they left the house together between ten and eleven o'clock that morning.[42]

The Cincinnati *Enquirer* (quoting the Jefferson *Journal* newspaper from April 12, 1877) reported their next actions: "Stopping at Kate Wood's restaurant on Austin Street, they drank one or two bottles of beer. The woman exhibited suspicions of her companion, and refused to permit him to pour out the beer or to handle her glass. Her conduct toward him was strange. He tried to procure a lunch from Mrs. Wood's, but failing to get what he desired, he went over to Henriques' restaurant on Polk street, and returned with a cooked chicken, sandwiches, pickles, etc, and two bottles of beer."[43]

The gentleman next went to a livery stable, where he attempted to rent a horse and buggy. Spillings, the liveryman, was not satisfied that he could provide for the safe return of the hack. Monroe offered to put up a $20 deposit, but the liveryman didn't think that it would be enough; Spillings would not give Monroe the rig. As he left in a huff, A. Monroe said, "I guess, then, that we can walk."[44]

So walk they did – the couple traversed the footbridge across Big Cypress Bayou to the west of the turning basin.[45]

A man named John Neff, a saloonkeeper in town, was coming into Jefferson at about 11 A.M. that morning, where he

[41] "Diamond Bessie Is Marion County's Most Famous Murder Case," Jefferson *Daily Jimplecute* April 11, 1937, p 6
[42] Ex Parte Abe Rothschild, Court of Appeals of Texas, 2 Tex. Ct. App. 560; 1877 Tex. Crim. App. Lexis 188, p.2.
[43] "Abe Rothschild: His Arrival in Jefferson, Texas," Cincinnati *Enquirer*, April 17, 1877, p. 2.
[44] Op.cit., Ex Parte Abe Rothschild, p.2.
[45] Tarpley, Fred. *Jefferson: Riverport to the Southwest*. Wolfe City, TX: Henington Pulishing Co. 1983.

met "A. Monroe and wife" leaving town on the bridge. It is entirely possible that John Neff was the last person to see Diamond Bessie alive.[46]

About two or three o'clock in the afternoon, Turner, the landlord of the Brooks House, saw A. Monroe come into the parlor of the hotel – his wife was not with him. Turner asked him if he had plans for dinner, and Monroe told him that he had already dined at Kate Wood's restaurant. Later, Monroe asked Mr. Turner if his wife had returned, and the hotelkeeper replied that he hadn't, but asked where she would be returning from. Monroe said that he had gone across the bayou to visit with some friends, and that she had stayed behind for a while.[47]

Monroe remained at the Brooks House the next day, Monday, and left by the east-bound train about three o'clock Tuesday morning, the 23rd. He had with him the trunk and valise with which the couple had arrived.[48]

H.J. Donovan, the depot baggage-master, saw Monroe with the same trunk as he was leaving town, and in fact, checked it through to Little Rock, Arkansas.[49]

The train on which Monroe left Jefferson was the first east-bound passenger train since he was last seen in the company of his wife on Sunday, January 21. It was, in effect, the first opportunity that he had to get out of town.[50]

---

[46] Ex Parte Abe Rothschild, Court of Appeals of Texas, 2 Tex. Ct. App. 560; 1877 Tex. Crim. App. Lexis 188, p.2.
[47] Ibid.
[48] Ibid.
[49] Ibid, p.3.
[50] Ibid, p.2.

The Coroner's Inquest

The victim had been dressed in a style, fashion, and quality of clothing not usually seen in Jefferson. She wore a black velvet hat with trim; silk stockings with a blue flower design in front; a pair of garters that were alike in design but one blue and one white, each fastened with patent metallic buckles; a chemise of linen; a plain white undershirt; flannel petticoat; black silk skirt; woolen basque and polonaise; very heavy black cloak with lap-over braid for the buttons (called a walking cloak); a collar; purple necktie; and kid (goat skin) shoes. The coroner gave a statement that she wore what he called a "nondescript." When asked what that was, he replied, "I do not know what it is and can't name it."[51]

---

[51] Walters, Mahlon L. "Who Done It to Whom?" Texas Bar Journal, 1963, p. 3.

Four women had been given the responsibility of disrobing the body and then dressing it in newly-made clothing for burial. One of the women in attendance was Isabella Gouldy, and another was Mollie Turk.[52]

Within twelve hours after being taken to the coroner's office, decomposition progressed rapidly and had become very considerable by the time of interment.

A coroner's inquest was held in the following days to examine the facts of the crime, and by that time the murdered woman had been identified by several witnesses. Dr. J.G. Eason said that he remembered her to be the same person who had been in the company of her husband, A. Monroe. A man named Frank Malloy viewed the corpse at the inquest, and recognized it as that of a woman he had seen about two weeks before at Mrs. Kate Wood's restaurant dining with her husband. D.P. McMullen saw the woman on Austin Street in Jefferson with A. Monroe on Sunday, January 21.[53]

Jennie Simpson, the chambermaid at the Brooks House, identified the body as that of the woman who arrived with A. Monroe and stayed in Room 4. She also related the story of the fighting that went on between the couple in that room. According to Simpson, the clothes presented by the coroner were the ones that the woman wore when she left the hotel with her husband on the morning of Sunday the 21st. The woman was also wearing two diamond rings. Later in the day, A. Monroe returned alone, and Jennie asked about his wife. He told her that they had been to dinner at Kate Wood's restaurant, and that she had remained there and would be back later. At that time, Monroe was wearing the two diamond rings that Jennie had seen earlier. The chambermaid was not aware of her

[52] Walters, Mahlon L. "Who Done It to Whom?" Texas Bar Journal, 1963, p. 3.
[53] Ex Parte Abe Rothschild, Court of Appeals of Texas, 2 Tex. Ct. App. 560; 1877 Tex. Crim. App. Lexis 188, p.3.

return that evening, but did hear Monroe pacing his room off and on all night long. Sometime during the night, he burned a pile of written papers in the fireplace.[54]

Simpson continued with the information that the next morning, Monroe did not want breakfast but asked her for a cup of coffee, saying that he had been sick the night before. He stayed in his room all day, and that evening Simpson inquired about his wife again. Monroe replied that she would meet him the next morning at the train.[55]

A man named W.A. Walker identified the deceased woman as someone that he had seen with her husband on a train from Marshall, Texas to Jefferson on January 19. He noted that she wore two unusually fine diamond rings on her fingers.[56]

H.J. Donovan, the baggage-master of the Texas & Pacific Railroad at Jefferson, had unloaded a trunk for the couple marked "A. Moore, N.O." when they arrived in town, and then checked the same trunk through to Little Rock, Arkansas for the man when he departed alone on Tuesday, January 23.[57]

With the testimony of other witnesses who had seen the deceased woman with the man known as A. Monroe in Jefferson, a sequence of events was constructed:

- A. Monroe and wife arrived in Jefferson by train from Marshall on Friday, January 19, 1877.
- The couple was seen around town by a number of citizens during their stay, wearing fine clothes and the lady sporting diamond jewelry.

---

[54] Ex Parte Abe Rothschild, Court of Appeals of Texas, 2 Tex. Ct. App. 560; 1877 Tex. Crim. App. Lexis 188, p.2.
[55] Ibid.
[56] Ibid.
[57] Ibid.

- They argued extensively behind closed doors at the Brooks House during their stay.
- The couple was last seen late Sunday morning, January 21, walking across the bridge over Big Cypress Bayou into the woods with a picnic basket. It was the last time that the woman was seen alive.
- A. Monroe was later back at the Brooks House Sunday afternoon wearing the rings that had been seen on his wife's hand. He first said that his wife had lingered at Kate Wood's restaurant, but when she didn't return that evening, amended his story to say that she would be meeting him at the train on Tuesday morning.
- A. Monroe left town alone the morning of Tuesday, January 23, with his wife's trunk.
- The woman's dead body was found approximately two weeks later in the woods south of Jefferson with a gunshot wound to the head.

Based on these known facts, Justice Bickford issued a warrant of arrest:

To the Sheriff or any Constable of Marion County: Greeting
Wheras on the 5th day of February A.D. 1877, a jury of inquest was held in said County of Marion before me, C.C. Beckford, a Justice of the Peace and exofficio coroner thereof upon the body of an unknown woman then and there lying dead:

And whereas it was found by the verdict of said jury, thereupon made up that on the 21st day of January A.D. 1877 in said county A. Monroe killed the said unknown woman and is therefore guilty of the crime of murder, you are therefore hereby commanded in the name of the State of Texas to take the body of the said A. Monroe if to be found in your county and forthwith bring him before me at my office in the City of

Jefferson in said County, then and there to be examined concerning the crime of murder, whereof he is charged as aforesaid and to be further dealt with as the law directs.

Herein fail not but have you then and there this warrant with your action there on as the law requires.

Given under my hand and official signature. This 6th day of February A.D. 1877.

(signed) C.C. Beckford

J.P. and ExOfficio Coronor of Marion County, Texas

The hunt for "A. Monroe" was on.

Bringing Rothschild Back

Following the information that A. Monroe and his wife traveled to Jefferson from Marshall, it was discovered that the couple arrived in Marshall on January 17 and stayed at the Capitol Hotel for two days. From there they travelled to Jefferson on January 19 on the "accommodation train," which served the two cities.[58]

The manager of the Capitol Hotel, C.H. Pepper, recognized the man from the description of A. Monroe as the person who had checked into his hotel. In Marshall, however, the couple had signed the register as, "A. Rothschild and wife, Cin'ti, O."[59]

---

[58] "Diamond Bessie Case One of Most Notorious in Texas History," Jefferson *Jimplecute*, June 17, 1965.

[59] Ex Parte Abe Rothschild, Court of Appeals of Texas, 2 Tex. Ct. App. 560; 1877 Tex. Crim. App. Lexis 188, p. 2.

Signature of "A. Rothschild [&] Wife Cinti, O"
from the register of the Capitol Hotel, Marshall

Signature of "A. Monroe [&] Wife StLouis, Mo"
from the register of the Brooks House, Jefferson

From this information and records that were supplied by railroad officials, it was determined that A. Monroe was actually Abraham Rothschild of Cincinnati, Ohio. He was the son of a wealthy family whose stately name had been known in the business world for generations, tracing back to the great banking houses of Europe.[60]

Rothschild had returned to Cincinnati from Jefferson, and he went about his business as usual acting in much the same manner as he did before. He frequented gambling establishments and brothels, although many thought that he seemed to be nervous and frightened. Rothschild imagined that someone was following him to kill him, and would frequently ask people if they saw the man who was shadowing him.[61]

On the 17th of February, he was in Aug's Clubhouse, and he asked somebody there whether they saw the man that was following him. Rothschild had a number of drinks that day, and

---

[60] Russell, Traylor. *The Diamond Bessie Murder and the Rothschild Trials.* Waco, Texas: Texian Press. 1971.

[61] "Abe Rothschild Convicted of Murder in the First Degree – The Story of the Killing of Diamond Bessie," The Cincinnati *Daily Enquirer*, December 25, 1878.

about 2:30 AM, he left the bar and sat on the steps. A few moments afterward, patrons inside heard a gunshot just outside the door. Fred, the bartender, along with Private Watchman Schwegman, dashed outside and found Rothschild sitting there with a pool of blood at his feet and a pistol by his side. The bullet had entered back of the right temple, passed diagonally forward, behind and through the orbit of the right eye, and lodged under the bridge of the nose. He said a tall man with black whiskers had shot him, although the wound appeared to be certainly self-inflicted. Rothschild was taken to his home, where a surgeon was called; most believed that his wound would be fatal.[62]

Meanwhile, back in Jefferson, a new warrant was issued for Abe Rothschild by Justice Bickford and telegraphed to the authorities in Cincinnati where he was arrested while recovering from the gunshot wound. Rothschild refused to voluntarily return to Texas, so an appeal was made to Governor Richard B. Hubbard for a warrant of extradition, which he immediately issued and sent to the Governor of Ohio.[63]

A few days later, the Indianapolis *News* reported: *The Cincinnati police have succeeded in finding the trunk of clothing belonging to Bessie Moore, for whose murder in Texas Abe Rothschild was arrested. The trunk was in the baggage room at one of the railroad depots where it had been sent by Rothschild.*[64]

Governor Hubbard appointed John M. Vines, the former Sheriff of Marion County, to travel to Cincinnati to bring Abe Rothschild back to Texas to stand trial. Three other men went with Vines: Deputy Sheriff G.W. Stroll, Marion County

---

[62] "Mysterious Shooting – Was it Assassination or Attempted Suicide?" The Cincinnati *Enquirer*, February 17, 1877, p. 4.

[63] Russell, Traylor. *The Diamond Bessie Murder and the Rothschild Trials.* Waco, Texas: Texian Press. 1971.

[64] The Indianapolis *News*, Indianapolis, Indiana, February 26, 1877.

Attorney Edward Guthridge, and Dr. J.H. Turner. Turner owned the Brooks House, and had picked Abe and Bessie up in his carriage when they first arrived in Jefferson; he was there to assist in the identification of Rothschild.[65]

When the men arrived in Cincinnati, Rothschild was identified immediately, but his family hired an attorney to try to block extradition.[66]

The Cincinnati *Enquirer* newspaper carried the story of the extradition hearing on March 7, 1877:

Abe Rothschild – The Questions of His Identity and the Legality of His Arrest

The announcement in the papers that the Rothschild matter would be heard before the Courts yesterday brought together a large crowd of curiosity-seekers of a grade different from that which ordinarily assembles in the Criminal Courtroom and much larger. A few ladies happened to be in the room by the reason of the fact that they were witnesses in a divorce case that was pending. A number of clerks from adjoining rooms of the Courthouse and persons from neighboring stores thronged into see what was to be seen. A number of policemen and detectives were also in the room, connected with the case in some manner as witnesses. A number of relatives of the defendant were also present, among them his father and uncle and one or two cousins. There was quite a sprinkling of Jews among the number, of which race the defendant is one, as his name implies. So great was the crowd that the presence of a Deputy Sheriff was rendered necessary to keep the passageways clear. This, however, was only done by packing the crowd into the space back of the bar, like cattle

---

[65] Russell, Traylor. *The Diamond Bessie Murder and the Rothschild Trials.* Waco, Texas: Texian Press. 1971, p. 29.
[66] Ibid, p. 30.

in the cars. After the proceedings had begun it was impossible to restrain the crowd, and they broke through the prescribed limits and filled the bar to overflowing.

At a few minutes after two o'clock, the prisoner was brought into Court, leaning on the arm of Officer Chumley, his right eye bandaged with a neat white handkerchief, and face of a pale ashy hue. He was dressed neatly in a suit of black, and his person was conspicuously devoid of jewelry. He was given a seat by his attorney, Major Blackburn. He stared about him for a little while, and then fixed his gaze on the ceiling in front of him, from which he did not remove his eyes, except to glance away, and then back again. The proceedings had not gone very far, until his physician, Dr. Davis, who attended him in Court, stated to Judge Avery that his patient was becoming weak from the excitement, and asked permission to remove him to the jail. The counsel for neither party objecting, the prisoner was taken into the prosecutor's office, and laid on a lounge. Subsequently he was taken to the jail and given a room in the women's quarters.

On the opening of the case Mr. Baker read the requisition made upon Governor Hayes, the warrant of the Governor for the arrest of the prisoner directed to the Sheriff of Hamilton County, and the affidavit upon which the requisition was ordered. The latter was signed by C.C. Blickford at Jefferson, Texas, and charged that A. Moore, alias A. Monroe, alias Abe Rothschild, murdered a woman unknown to the affiant on the 21st of January, 1877, in Marion County, Texas.

The Prosecutor then stated that the authority to receive the defendant was issued to John M. Vines who was in Court ready to receive the prisoner and convey him back to Texas. He desired to call Mr. Vines for the purpose of identifying the prisoner.

Major Blackburn, at this point, stated that after the submission of the documentary evidence he desired to submit a motion to exclude the introduction of any further evidence, and also motions to quash the entire proceedings and for the discharge of the prisoner.

At this stage of the case the prisoner was removed from the court as stated above.

The Court suggested that it would be better for M. Blackburn to argue his motions at conclusion of the testimony to be offered by the Prosecution, stating at this stage only the grounds of the motions.

Major Blackburn stated that the principal grounds of the motion were: First that the affidavit upon which the Governor issued his warrant was not sufficient in law to authorize him to issue his warrant or requisition; second, that the warrant or requisition of the Governor of Texas upon the Governor of Ohio was, for the reasons first stated, absolutely void, that the warrant from the Governor of Ohio to the Sheriff of Hamilton County for the arrest of the prisoner for the same reasons, was void absolutely, and likewise the authority attempted to be delegated by the Governor of Texas to the agent representing that State to receive, if it should be so ordered, the prisoner from this Court, for the reasons stated, was void and without authority of law.

The Court then inquired what testimony the Prosecutor desired to offer, and was informed that it was such as should identify the person authorized by the authorities of Texas to receive the prisoner, and after that testimony as to the identity of the person at the bar with that of the person mentioned in the requisition.

John M. Vines was then called and examined as follows:

"I live in Jefferson, Marion County, Texas; I am a merchant there; have been Sheriff of the county; I am the person named in the commission of the Governor of Texas; I received the commission from Governor Hubbard to receive the person named herein."

Q. "Was the person whom you saw brought to the bar of the Court today the person mentioned in the authority?"
A. It is, sir."

Q. "Did you see the defendant in Marion County, Texas, in the early part of the year?"
A. Yes, sir; he is the same person."

Q. "Under what name was he known there?"
A. He had two aliases there, A. Monroe and Munroe. He registered at the hotel as A. Monroe. He is the person named in the requisition and in the order of arrest, and also in the affidavit of Bickford."

Cross-examined: Received the order from the Governor.

Q. "Did you make the application in person?"
A. No, sir. I suppose it was issued to me under a petition we presented to the Governor. I received it here in Cincinnati."

Q. "Do you not know who sent it to you?"
A. It was sent by the Secretary. I have a letter to that effect."

Q. "Were you in Texas when the application was presented to the Governor for the allowance of the requisition?"
A. I was. The affidavit in this case is a copy of the one made by Bickford."

Q. "Had any indictment been found against the prisoner in Texas?"
A. No, sir."

Q. "Were you present when Bickford made the affidavit?"

41

A. No, sir. Neither I nor the Prosecutor from Texas made any affidavits in the case; neither did Dr. Turner, who accompanied us here. So far as I know this is the only paper that was presented to the Governor upon which he issued his warrant. There was a petition sent to the Governor of Texas praying that a reward be given for the arrest of the prisoner. There was no other sworn affidavit to my knowledge."

Q. "Did you accompany Mr. Guthridge, the Prosecutor, from your State to Columbus to obtain the requisition from Governor Hayes?"
A. Yes, sir. Colonel Lee, Private Secretary of the Governor, ordered the requisition filled up. The man who drew it up handed it to me. I was in the office of the Governor all the time, and did not see the Governor".

Mr. Baker objected to testimony tending to show that the requisition was not ordered by the Governor, claiming that the paper was in Court, and must speak for itself.

Major Blackburn: "I propose to prove that the Governor was not present, and that the issuing of the paper was the work of somebody else not having authority in law to issue it."

The Court: "The warrant is conclusive that it was issued by the Governor. It is a matter of record. The only hesitation I have is whether I should shut you out from proving what you can by the witness or whether I should allow you to take exceptions with the advantage of this statement that you propose to prove something which perhaps you will not be able to prove by this witness."

Major Blackburn: "With the testimony already submitted by the witness I feel it incumbent on me not only to make the statement, but to submit each and every question and solicit an answer and have the question overruled. I would prefer to get the testimony on record so that the reviewing Court, if the case should get before them, may have the full facts before them, and let this question be put to rest, inasmuch as the Courts of the different States have varied in their views upon the question. It is a question of vital importance to the prisoner at the bar."

The Court: "Put any question you choose, and I will pass upon it at the objections of the Prosecutor."

Major Blackburn asked a great number of questions of the witness as to how and by whom the warrant was issued which directed the Sheriff of this county to make the arrest of the prisoner, and how and by whom the requisition was conveyed to Governor Hayes and the warrant to the Sheriff.

The Court held that it is a matter of no moment whatever how the affidavit got to Columbus. We have the official act of the officers certifying that it was filed there, and that act is certified to by the great seal of the State.

Major Blackburn: "You understand I want to raise the point in every conceivable way for the purpose of getting exceptions, and Your Honor will not feel offended at my repeating the question in so many different shapes."

*Q. "You said that the prisoner was the man who registered at the hotel in Jefferson; are you familiar with his handwriting?"
A. I don't think I ever saw him write his name. I did not see him register at the hotel."*

Q. "Then all you know is what somebody else told you?"

43

A. I saw the signature that was said to be his. "

Q. "You do not know of your own knowledge that he registered there?"
A. I did not see him register. "

Q. "Did you ever see Rothschild in your city?"
A. Yes, sir; on January last, sometime between the 18th and the 21st. He was stopping at the Brooks House. "

Q. "Did you see him there?"
A. I met him on the street. I knew he was at the Brooks house by his name being on the register. "

Q. "Did you see Rothschild's name there?"
A. No, sir. I saw Monroe's name there. I was told that he registered there. "

Re-direct Examination:
Q. "How did you come to go to the hotel to inspect that signature?"
A. I went with the Chief of Police and other citizens there. We, of course, suspected this man of committing the murder. "

The Court: "Ask the witness to tell how he identified the person. "

The Witness: "I met the man on the street frequently. It is a small place, and everybody notices a stranger coming to town. He was in company with a very attractive young woman, who had some very flashy jewelry, which is a rather uncommon thing in our country. Afterward, the woman, with whom the prisoner was with, was found dead. "

Q. "By Mr. Baker – Was the woman who was found dead the same as the woman whom you saw with him alive?"
A. Yes, sir; I saw her dead."

Q. "Did she have any jewelry on at that time?"

Major Blackburn objected to the question. The State claimed it was asked for the purpose of identifying the woman. The question was, however, withdrawn.

Q. "How long before you saw her dead was it that you saw her alive?"
A. About eight or ten days."

Q. "How many times did you see her in company with defendant?"
A. Four or five times, but they were promenading about the streets, and I met them frequently during the day. I did not see them in their hotel. I saw them on the streets and in the stores. I did not know the name of the man."

Q. "Did you make inquiry?

Objected to –

The Court: "The object of the inquiry is to ascertain whether the prisoner is the man meant to be charged. As part of the proof, the name by which he went in Texas is competent as one of the links of identification. And therefore the question is not whether this was his name, but whether he went by that name. The witness is competent to speak, because he lived in Texas and heard the man called by that name."

Major Blackburn: "I will ask Your Honor that the witness confine himself to information received antecedent to the date upon which the alleged offense was committed."

The Court: "Any information as to the name of the man or the name he went by prior to the filing of the affidavit, on the 17th of February, is competent."

The Witness: "The man went by the name of A. Monroe there. I obtained that information from hearsay. Persons would inquire who he was. He created some interest with our people there, being with a fancy and handsomely-dressed woman."

Q. "How do you connect the person you saw on the street with the name you saw on the register?"
A. By what Dr. Turner said about it and others who inquired his name."

Q. "How came you to go to the hotel?"
A. We had a curiosity to know who the man was. He acted a little singularly strolling around. Myself and several others went there. We inquired from Dr. Turner and the hotel clerk who that fellow was that was going around with that fancy woman with diamonds. After the body of the woman was found we went to the hotel. We all agreed that Rothschild was the one that did the deed. Dr. Turner returned home several days ago."

Re. Cross-Examination:

Q. "What prompted you to go to the hotel to see who they were?"
A. From the fact that they were a very remarkable looking couple for our country. He was a very fancy looking chap and

46

she was extraordinarily dressed. Curiosity at the time was the reason for our going."

Q. "Did you inquire about the business they were on?"
A. We made inquiry more particularly as to what business the woman was on. The woman more interested us than the man."

C. Wappenstein, sworn: "Am a policeman. Captain Johnson and I arrested the prisoner; his name is Abe Rothschild. I visited him in company with Dr. Turner of Texas at his home on Fifth Street."

Q. "Did Turner identify him as being Abe Monroe?"

Major Blackburn objected to the question, saying that the prisoner was at that time lying in a semi-unconscious condition from the effect of a bullet having passed through his brain.

The Court: "Ask him whether or not Dr. Turner had any conversation with the prisoner."
A. Dr. Davis held the prisoner up and Rothschild kept saying, 'Do not hurt me.' I think he was conscious at the time."

Q. "State any conversation that Dr. Turner had with the prisoner."
A. Dr. Turner simply nodded and the prisoner shook his head."

Mr. Vines was recalled to testify as to how he connected the dead woman with the woman mentioned in the affidavit. He stated that she was registered as the wife of Monroe, but the common talk was that she was a prostitute traveling with him.

47

The case was then argued on the sufficiency of the papers and laid over until this morning for the purpose or argument on the question of the identity of the prisoner.[67]

Rothschild had a very good reason to fight the extradition. On March 4, the Dallas *Daily Herald* newspaper reported:

The sentiment of the Jefferson people in the matter is almost unanimous – that hanging is almost too good for the woman murderer, and that a slow fire should be started under him. Cooler counsels, however, will undoubtedly prevail, but it is pretty certain that if Abe Rothschild is brought back to Jefferson from Cincinnati, he will not escape a felon's death.[68]

The matter had been settled by March 19, when John Vines sent a telegraph to the mayor of Jefferson stating, "The case of Abe Rothschild, the murderer of Bessie Moore, has been decided in our favor in the court with stay of delivery for twenty days. We leave tonight for Jefferson."[69]

The twenty day delay was ordered by the Ohio court because Rothschild's attorney argued that he was not well enough to travel after his attempted suicide. The attending physician made the following statement: "I, O.E. Davis, physician and surgeon, attendant physician upon Abe Rothschild, certify that his present condition is such that he could not, without endangering his life, be removed from the hospital, and will not be able to be removed for some days, under the most favorable circumstances."[70]

---

[67] "Abe Rothschild – The Questions of His Identity and the Legality of His Arrest," The Cincinnati *Inquirer*, Cincinnati, Ohio Wednesday, March 7, 1877, p. 8.
[68] "Notes by the Way," The Dallas *Daily Herald*, Dallas, Texas, March 4, 1877, p. 2.
[69] Russell, Traylor. *The Diamond Bessie Murder and the Rothschild Trials.* Waco, Texas: Texian Press, 1971, p. 30.
[70] "Abe Rothschild: The Testimony as to His Condition," The Cincinnati *Enquirer*, Cincinnati, Ohio, March 4, 1877, p. 1.

As to his stay at the hospital, the Cincinnati *Enquirer* reported:

Abe Rothschild is playing possum at the Cincinnati Hospital, and trying his best to induce his attendants to believe that he is not in his right mind at times. His efforts are very lame, however, and are too palpably made for effect to have the desired result. Besides, he will not be tried here, but in Texas, where it only takes nine of the twelve jurymen to convict – and lunacy is not a valid defense down there. At the request of the police authorities, Miss Frank Wright and one of her girls, who know Bessie Moore well when she was here, visited the Superintendent's office yesterday afternoon, and inspected the contents of the trunk of the murdered woman. They recognized all in it as the property of the deceased, except a few dresses which she had bought after leaving this city. Rothschild will probably start for Texas about the middle of next week.[71]

When the twenty-day waiting period had expired, John Vines and Deputy Sheriff Stroll returned to Cincinnati to collect the prisoner.[72]

The Oakland Tribune newspaper gave the following report on April 5:

Cincinnati: In the case of Abe Rothschild, who is accused of having murdered Bessie Moore at Jefferson, Texas, and is here awaiting extradition proceedings, Judge Watson this morning dismissed the writ of habeas corpus. Sheriff Wallace, on the advice of the attorneys, turned Rothschild over to the Texan authorities in obedience to the order of Judge Avery.[73]

---

[71] "Abe Rothschild," The Cincinnati *Enquirer*, Cincinnati, Ohio, Feb 28, 1877, p. 8.

[72] Russell, Traylor. *The Diamond Bessie Murder and the Rothschild Trials.* Waco, Texas: Texian Press. 1971, p. 30.

[73] "Texas Murderer Extradited," Oakland *Tribune*, Oakland, California, April 5, 1877, p. 3.

On April 5, John Vines and Deputy Stroll quietly escorted him to a carriage that they had standing by at the corner of Broadway and Sycamore streets, near the entrance to the jail. They drove him quickly to Lawrenceburg, Indiana where they could leave on a train for Jefferson without any interference from Rothschild's attorney or friends.[74]

As the train carrying the lawmen and the accused murderer stopped briefly in Texarkana, Texas, a reporter noted:

Rothschild, the alleged murderer of Bessie Moore, killed at Jefferson some time ago, passed through here this morning, en route to Jefferson. The prisoner is in charge of John M. Vines, who had to use some adroitness to get him out of reach of Cincinnati friends and to avoid legal embarrassments. Rothschild is cheerful; is a fine looking fellow of twenty-two years of age, and the son of a very wealthy merchant of Cincinnati. He was run into Indiana before his people were aware of his removal.[75]

At about 1:00 PM on April 7, the train pulled into the station at Jefferson. Several hundred people were at the depot to witness the arrival. Curiosity seemed to be the motivating factor, since there were no signs of violence or insults toward the prisoner by the crowd. Rothschild seemed somewhat embarrassed when he first beheld the large crowd and showed signs of uneasiness. The city had a strong police force on hand in case an attempt was made to take the prisoner from the authorities, but there was no incident. He was unceremoniously

---

[74] "Extradited: Abe Rothschild, the Reported Murderer of Bessie Moore, Remanded to the Texas Authorities," The *Daily Milwaukee News*, April 6, 1877.

[75] "Abe Rothschild's Return: Arrival of the Alleged Perpetrator of the Jefferson Woman Murder." Galveston *Daily News*, Galveston, Texas, April 8, 1877.

turned over to Sheriff Bagby, and transported to the county jail in a closed carriage.[76]

The crowd drifted to the jail in small groups, some standing outside into the night hoping for another glimpse of Rothschild.[77]

The cells of the jail were on the upper floor – four rooms, well ventilated, each having an eight by ten foot iron cage inside. Rothschild was confined to one of these rooms, and locked into the cell when it was time for bed. A single guard slept in the room outside of the iron cage.[78]

The next day people came into town by foot and on mules, and spent hours lounging around the jail exchanging views on the matter. A reporter wrote, "I went out there about eleven o'clock, in company with General Malloy, the Collector of Internal Revenue, and was at once admitted to Rothschild's cell. I found him seated on his bed, which consisted of a single (or narrow) mattress laid on the floor, and furnished with clean sheets, quilts and large feather pillow, covered with an exquisitely-worked pillowcase. He was in fine spirits, laughed over the report that he had been kidnapped [from Ohio by John Vines], and said that no man could have been more kindly treated than he had."[79]

The next day the same reporter went back to the cell, and wrote, "Today I again visited the jail, and making my way through a crowd, went up to his cell. I found two ladies seated within, one of whom had a young child, which Rothschild had in his arms, and was playing with, with all the adroitness of an

---

[76] "Abe Rothschild's Return: Arrival of the Alleged Perpetrator of the Jefferson Woman Murder." Galveston *Daily News*, Galveston, Texas April 8, 1877.

[77] "Abe Rothschild: His Arrival at Jefferson," The Cincinnati *Enquirer*, Cincinnati, Ohio, April 14, 1877, p. 5.

[78] Ibid.

[79] Ibid.

expert. A neat, new bedstead, stand, table, chairs, and bathtub had been purchased by him and placed in the cell. A beautiful bouquet of fresh roses and evergreens ornamented the table, while various evidences of attention to comfort and convenience were apparent. When the ladies retired, I entered into conversation with him, and found that he was in the same apparent good spirits in which I found him yesterday. He said he had not indicated the line of his defense to anyone, and would not, as that matter belonged entirely to his counsel. He would admit that he was in town at the time charged that he was here, but nothing more. I then showed him a photograph of the register at the Brooks House, when he remarked, 'By George, that is correct.' He then made some other statements, which he subsequently requested should not be published, as they might injure his case, and which I omit."[80]

A week after his arrival, Abe reportedly wrote a letter to a friend in Cincinnati:

Jefferson Tex, Apl 14 77.

Dear Friend

I arrived here safely one week ago today; am well and trust you can safely say same as regards yourself. I am getting along very well here, in fact much more pleasantly than I did at [Cincinnati]. I have a very nice, large well ventilated room here with every comfort that I could ask for. I am allowed to promenade the streets twice a day, an hour in the A.M. and one in the P.M. Everybody is very kind and courteous to me and all seem bent to make me feel like anything but a prisoner.

My visitors number all the way from 50 to 300 daily; they are thinning down considerably now. I am presented with 4 or 5 bouquets daily, in fact yesterday I received 6 from the girls

---

[80] "Abe Rothschild: His Arrival at Jefferson," The Cincinnati *Enquirer*, Cincinnati, Ohio, April 14, 1877, p. 5.

and ladies of the town. The jailer is one of the boys, and I am permitted to have the society of ladies whenever I please. I was very sorry that I did not get the opportunity to say goodbye to you and my friends in the jail.

I think I shall have an operation performed on that defunct eye of mine and have a blue glass eye chucked in. My father and cousin arrived here yesterday. As far as my case is concerned, I am positive it will terminate all okay and it scarcely troubles my mind, or rather I never think of it unless my attention is drawn to it. It will take a little time, though. The preliminary trial comes off next Tuesday.

What is the news at home, how are Ike, Mike and Frank getting along? Let me know. Everything is nice and green down here as far as vegetation is concerned, not so though as regards the people. It seems very strange for the Northern people to think that Texas people are different from those of any other section of the country. This is a wrong impression. I don't want to be with a more clever set. As regards myself, I wanted to come down here in the first place, but then the old man was afraid on account of the rumors afloat regarding the wild "Texans." News that would interest you I have nothing of. Please extend my kindest regards to Mr. Porter, Dan McCarty, "The Turk," also Frank, Ike, and Mike. Would be pleased to hear from you shortly. I remain with thanks for your kind attention shown me, your friend.

Abe Rothschild

P. S. – Address care G.W. Stoll, Jefferson, Texas.[81]

---

[81] "Abe Rothschild: The Sweet Pet of the Texans," The Cincinnati *Enquirer*, Cincinnati, Ohio, April 18, 1877, p. 8.

Rothschild on Trial

After spending a number of days in the Jefferson jail, it was time for Abe to have his day in court. On April 17, 1877, the preliminary examination of Rothschild was, by the agreement of counsel, deferred until the 25th. There was an array of counsel present on both sides, and the courtroom was crowded with spectators, who seemed to take a lively interest in the case. According to accounts, "The prisoner appears very confident of an acquittal, and asserts that he is innocent of the charge preferred against him. Nothing new has been elicited in the case."[82]

---

[82] "Abe Rothschild: The Sweet Pet of the Texans," The Cincinnati *Enquirer*, Cincinnati, Ohio, April 18, 1877, p. 8.

On April 18, 1877 The Cincinnati *Enquirer* gave the following account:

The courtroom yesterday was crowded. Every available space occupied. That morbid curiosity which we find exhibited everywhere was manifested here. There was a feverish desire to get a sight of the prisoner, and, when after a few moments, the proceedings were ended and he was remanded to jail, there was an evident feeling of disappointment. No murder trial in Texas has ever excited more public interest. This is not surprising. The deed itself was revolting and, when with it are connected the strange circumstances with which it is invested, it was calculated to shock the moral sense of the community.

The prisoner was represented by the six distinguished lawyers mentioned before, and to these was added Colonel W.L. Crawford, a brilliant attorney from Dallas, formerly a resident of Jefferson. The difficulty about the prosecution has been that the State makes no provision for employing anyone to assist the County Attorney [Edward Guthridge]. He is a young man, and, without desiring to disparage him, by no means qualified to meet such an array of experience and talent. There is too much interest felt in the case, however, to permit it to go off in this manner. Money has been raised by subscription, and other counsel engaged. The County Attorney was reinforced by Colonel M.L. Lewis of Red River, and Captain George T. Todd of this city. Major Stedman, of Marshall, will be the leading counsel for the State. Other lawyers of distinction will also probably take part; among them Colonel W.B. Wright of Paris, and several from Marshall are spoken of.

The evidence against Rothschild, it is true, is circumstantial, but is so connected that it appears conclusive. How he will meet it no one knows, or can conjecture. The only favorable circumstance, if such it is made to appear, is the length of time that the woman laid in the woods. It was fifteen days before the body was found, and even then, strange to say, there was scarcely any visible signs of decomposition. But can he tell what he did with her? How he came by her rings? Why he left Jefferson without her, taking with him her trunk and clothing? Can he account for his conflicting statements in Texas and elsewhere? These explained, his prompt acquittal will be secured.[83]

As noted in the previous newspaper article, the prosecution team was slight when compared to the defense hired by Rothschild's family, prompting Texas Governor Richard Bennett Hubbard to appoint special counsel to aid the State, specifically B.H. Epperson and T.J. Campbell, both of Jefferson. The Galveston *Daily News* responded to this action with a question that in our world today would be unthinkably politically incorrect. The paper mused, "What prompted this action on the part of Governor Hubbard? Was it partiality for prostitutes, or his antipathy for the Jews?"[84]

Taking the opposite view, the Austin *Weekly Statesman* wrote, "Governor Hubbard proposes to suppress crime in Texas, and while certain selfish partisan papers criticize his conduct because he employed able counsel to prosecute Abe Rothschild, the Jefferson murderer, we hope he will follow up the precedent thus wisely set until men learn that murdering is not a pleasant or profitable pastime in Texas."[85]

A Grand Jury had been impaneled and on April 26, 1877, returned the following indictment against Abe Rothschild:

In the name and by the authority of the State of Texas, the Grand Jurors of the State of Texas, duly elected, impaneled, sworn and charged to inquire into, and true presentment make,

---

[83] "Progress of the Abe Rothschild Murder Case," The Cincinnati *Enquirer*, Cincinnati, Ohio, April 22, 1877, p. 4.

[84] "State Press," The Galveston *Daily News*, Galveston, Texas, April 26, 1877, p. 3.

[85] "Governor Hubbard Proposes," The Austin *Weekly Statesman*, Austin, Texas, May 3, 1877, p. 2.

of all felonies, misdemeanors, committed in the county of Marion, in said State, cognizable in the District Court, held in and for the county of Marion and the State aforesaid, upon their oaths present, that on the 21ˢᵗ day of January, 1877, in the county of Marion and State aforesaid, one Abe Rothschild, late of said county, did unlawfully, feloniously, willfully, wickedly, and by force, and of his express malice and aforethought, the said Abe Rothschild being then and there possessed of sound memory and discretion, commit an assault, and with a certain pistol, the same being then and there a deadly weapon, loaded and charged with gunpowder and divers leaden bullets, in the right hand of the said Abe Rothschild, then and there had and held within shooting distance of the person of a certain woman, whose name to the Grand Jurors is unknown, and who was then and there a reasonable creature in the peace of God and our said State being he, the said Abe Rothschild, the muzzle of the said pistol at, to, against and upon the body of the unknown woman did present and the contents of one of the barrels of the pistol, he, the said Abe Rothschild, at, to, against and upon the person of the said unknown woman, did shoot, fire off and discharge giving into and inflicting upon the unknown woman by means of the gunpowder and bullet fired and discharged out of the pistol by the said Abe Rothschild as one mortal wound the dimensions and size of which wound is unknown to the Grand Jurors upon the left temple of the said unknown woman did then and there instantly die, and so the Grand Jurors upon their oaths do say that at the time and place aforesaid and by the use of the means aforesaid and under the circumstances aforesaid he, the said Abe Rothschild did kill and murder the said unknown woman against the peace and dignity of the State. – L.A. Ellis, Foreman of the Grand Jury[86]

---

[86] "Abraham Rothschild: The Grand Jury's Opinion," The Cincinnati *Enquirer*, Cincinnati, Ohio, May 2, 1877, p. 2.

Back in Jefferson, the initial indictment against Rothschild was found to be faulty, and on May 4 County Attorney Edward Guthride filed a motion of dismissal because it was defective and would not sustain a conviction. The dismissal was granted, and immediately returned to the Grand Jury. A second indictment was returned that same day.[87]

The trial began in earnest on May 24, 1877. According to the Cincinnati Enquirer, "The courtroom was crowded – all men. It is very rare here, under any circumstances, for ladies to appear in a courtroom. The prisoner was dressed with scrupulous care – black coat, light pants and vest, neat shirt with gold studs, and black necktie. He exhibits perfect self-reliance and quite indifference."[88]

The counsels for the prosecution in the case were T.J. Campbell, George T. Todd, S.H. Russell, Edward Guthridge, W.S. Coleman, and B.H. Epperson. The counsels for the defense were D.B. Culberson, Hec. McKay, H.P. Mabry, J.H. Culberson, W.T. Armistead, and M.L. Crawford.[89]

When the prosecution announced that they were ready for trial, the defense counsel moved to throw out the jury pool for three reasons:

1. The jury summonses were issued on the 8th for appearance on the 24th, but the court clerk made a clerical error instructing them to report on the 15th.
2. The jury pool list delivered by the sheriff to the defense team showed the entire pool from which the people were drawn, but should have been the pool of those specifically summoned for trial.

[87] Russell, Traylor. *The Diamond Bessie Murder and the Rothschild Trials.* Waco, Texas: Texian Press. 1971, p. 55.
[88] "For His Life: The Trial of Abe Rothschild," The Cincinnati *Enquirer*, Cincinnati, Ohio, May 25, 1877, p. 1.
[89] "Abe Rothschild's Trial," The Galveston *Daily News*, Galveston, Texas, May 25, 1877, p. 1.

3. The defendant should have been given a full day to examine the jury pool, but instead the list was only delivered on the day of the trial.

The arguments over these points lasted over four hours and involved all lawyers present. The prosecution contended that the jury list had actually been presented to Rothschild two days before, but the defense contended that it had not. The jailer, Mr. William Jefferson Fergusson, was called to testify on the matter but he could not conclusively remember when the jury list had been delivered, or by whom. After a full day, the court was dismissed until 9 a.m. the next morning. [90]

The next morning, the prosecution announced that it was ready for trial, but the defense asked Judge B.T. Estes for a recess because the defendant was not yet ready. Just after noon, the defense counsel asked for a continuance of trial to further prepare their defense. They hoped to prove Rothschild's innocence by the testimony of a man named Simon Hart, who allegedly saw a woman and a gentleman, a stranger, crossing the bayou in Jefferson. He would further testify that he saw the body of a dead woman on February 5, and it was not the one that Rothschild had been seen with. They also wanted to bring a witness named Alice Dumasky who would testify that she recognized the dead body as that of a woman named Alice Kirby, and that she even recognized the clothing that was on the body. They further planned on bringing a witness named Mollie Shannon who was allegedly a friend of Bessie Moore, who would testify that she had been pregnant, and had undergone an abortion that was followed by a long illness. Finally, the defense hoped to prove that the witnesses that the

---

[90] "Abe Rothschild's Trial," The Galveston *Daily News*, Galveston, Texas, May 25, 1877, p. 1.

State had brought in from Cincinnati were actually men of questionable repute.[91]

M.L. Crawford, attorney for defense, made the argument that the body that had been discovered in the woods could not be that of Bessie Moore, because it was evident to examining physicians that the woman had not been *enciente* [with child] in life. He stated that Abe Rothschild could conclusively prove that Bessie Moore had been *enceinte.*[92]

Arguments in court continued throughout the day. The prosecution maintained that whoever the woman might be, Bessie Moore or Alice Kirby, Abe Rothschild killed her on the 21st of January and left town on the 23rd. The defense asserted that they could prove that Bessie Moore was alive after January 21, that the murdered woman was someone else unacquainted with Rothschild, and he was therefore innocent. Both sides brought compelling statements, not completing until 8 p.m. that evening. Judge B.T. Estes immediately sustained the motion by the defense for continuance of the case, disposing of it until the next court term in May, 1878.[93]

Rothschild was returned to the jail in Jefferson, and his defense team continued to work on the case.

In Cincinnati, the police department collected the reward that had been posted for the capture of Abe Rothschild – $223.30. They gave it to the Cincinnati Police Relief Fund.[94]

---

[91] "The Rothschild Trial: An Interesting Case of Continuance – Proceedings in Court at Jefferson Yesterday," The Galveston Daily News, Galveston, Texas, May 26, 1877, p. 1.

[92] Ibid.

[93] "The Rothschild Trial: An Interesting Case of Continuance – Proceedings in Court at Jefferson Yesterday," The Galveston *Daily News*, Galveston, Texas, May 26, 1877, p. 1.

[94] "The Cincinnati Police Received Award," The Cincinnati *Enquirer*, Cincinnati, Ohio, June 23, 1877, p. 8.

HABEAS CORPUS

The Habeas Corpus Hearing & More

A writ of habeas corpus, also known as the "great writ," is a summons with the force of a court order; it is addressed to the custodian of a prisoner (a prison official, for example, or a district attorney) and demands that a prisoner be taken before the court, and that the custodian present proof of authority, allowing the court to determine whether the custodian has lawful authority to detain the prisoner. If the custodian is acting beyond his or her authority, then the prisoner must be released. Any prisoner, or another person acting on his or her behalf, may petition the court, or a judge, for a writ of habeas corpus.[95]

Rothschild's legal team filed a writ of habeas corpus on August 1, and he appeared in court on the morning of August 15, looking calm and collected. A petition for the prisoner was read, stating that he was unjustly and unlawfully held in prison.

---

[95] Venn Dicey, Albert. *Introduction to the Study of the Law of the Constitution*. London: Macmillan And Co., Limited, 1885.

Arguments on both the defense and prosecution argued into the evening, when the court finally adjourned.[96]

Judge B.T. Estes had sworn in several additional deputies for the protection of the prisoner because emotion in town was running high against Rothschild.[97]

One matter that came up in the hearing was the alleged plan of several Jefferson citizens to get Rothschild out of jail, and personally deal with him for the crime for which he was accused. One of the men supposedly part of the plan, P.M. Allen, was put on the stand to answer the accusations. He refused to answer any questions about it on the grounds that it might incriminate him.[98]

Arguments from both sides were wrapped up on August 30, and Judge B.T. Estes denied the writ, and Abe Rothschild was returned to the jail. The trial was set for November, 1877.[99]

Rothschild's lawyers appealed the writ of habeas corpus, which pushed out the actual hearing date. The Court of Appeals heard the case, and the finding was reported in the November 1, 1877 edition of the Galveston *Daily News*. "In the case of Abe Rothschild vs. the State of Texas, from Marion County, the decision of the lower court was affirmed."[100]

The decision of the appeals court read, "The facts of this case suffice of themselves to impress upon it a remarkable character, and have elicited a widespread interest of unusual intensity. With such a case in hand, it is safe to predict that the

---

[96] "Abe Rothschild: Brought Into Court on a Writ of Habeas Corpus – Arguments Partially Heard, and the Case Still On," The Cincinnati *Enquirer*, Cincinnati, Ohio, August 16, 1877.

[97] Russell, Traylor. *The Diamond Bessie Murder and the Rothschid Trials* (Waco: Texian Press, 1971), p. 65.

[98] Ibid., p. 66.

[99] Ibid.

[100] "Court of Appeals," The Galveston *Daily News*, Galveston, Texas, November 1, 1877.

eminent counsel engaged in it will not fail to make it a permanent landmark in the judicial annals of this country."[101]

The court also said, "The able counsel on both sides of the case have reflected honor and credit upon themselves and their profession by the force of their arguments and the ability of their briefs."[102]

When the appeal was finished, however, it simply meant that Abe Rothschild would stay in jail, and that the appeal of the writ of habeas corpus had delayed the actual trial.

One positive aspect of the appeal for Rothschild was that his defense team was able to see all of the State's evidence. In Abe's favor, the State had nothing but circumstantial evidence. Although over thirty witnesses were listed to testify about everything from the state of the body, to the weather prior to the discovery of the victim, to the sightings of Bessie Moore in Jefferson after Abe left town. The State's main evidence came from Jennie Simpson, a chambermaid at the Brooks House with her testimony about the couple's fighting in their room. The main witness for the defense was Isabella Gouldy.

While Rothschild was attempting to gain freedom via bail, work on the case against him was proceeding. One breakthrough was reported in the September 20, 1877 edition of the Cincinnati *Enquirer*, which said, "Rothschild will have a hard time beating justice. A detective from this city has made some discoveries in St. Louis very damaging to the "friend" of Bessie Moore.[103]

The Fort Wayne *Daily Gazette* in Indiana gave more specific detains:

---

[101] Russell, Traylor. *The Diamond Bessie Murder and the Rothschid Trials* (Waco: Texian Press, 1971), p. 67.
[102] Ibid.
[103] "Rothschild Will Have a Hard Time," The Cincinnati *Enquirer*, Cincinnati, Ohio, September 20, 1877, p. 4.

The Chain of Evidence Thickens

St. Louis, September 20 – An important link in the evidence against Abe Rothschild, of Cincinnati, charged with murdering Bessie Moore, at Jefferson, Texas, was found here yesterday by Detective Snelbaker of Cincinnati, who discovered in Walker's pawn broker shop on Olive Street, two diamond rings, pawned there six days after the murder, by Rothschild himself, who receipted for the money, and the receipts will be brought against him at trial.[104]

The *Times-Picayune* of New Orleans ran a story a few days later that seemed to seal the fate of Rothschild even more:

The Missing Link
Damning Testimony Against Abe Rothschild – Bessie Moore's Diamonds Found in a St. Louis Pawn Shop – Rothschild's Signature Attached to the Receipt for the Money Obtained Upon Them.

St. Louis, Sept. 19 – At last the terrible mystery which for so many months has shrouded the murder of Bessie Moore, at Jefferson, Texas, in January last, seems on the point of being solved. And the solution comes from a source entirely unexpected to those unacquainted with the inside history of that dark transaction. The witnesses in this case are dumb witnesses, but they speak in tones which must strike a chill of terror to the heart of the perpetrator of that cruel crime; and there is scarcely room for doubt that their testimony will send the murderer to a murderer's just doom.

For several days past Detective Tom Snelbaker, of Cincinnati, has been in this city, following up certain clues which he had obtained, and which he believed would tend to fasten the crime upon Abe Rothschild, now in a Jefferson jail

---

[104] "The Chain of Evidence Thickens," Fort Wayne *Daily Gazette*, Fort Wayne, Indiana, September 21, 1877, p. 1.

awaiting trial. Today he [Snelbaker] turned up what is supposed to be the sole necessary link in the chain of evidence which points unmistakably to Rothschild as the murderer – the diamonds which the woman wore at the time of the murder. In Walker's pawn shop Snelbaker found a register, page 229 of which contains these entries: Ticket 4267. One single-stone diamond ring; loaned $165. Ticket 4268. One seven-stone cluster diamond ring; loaned $185.

Both sums were loaned on January 25, six days after the murder, and Rothschild had receipted for the money with his own name. Snelbaker saw and identified the jewels. He has taken steps to secure the testimony from interference or abstraction. The whereabouts of these diamonds has heretofore been one of the difficulties with which the prosecution has had to contend. The mystery is at last solved; and when Abe Rothschild affixed his name to the receipt for the money obtained upon the murdered woman's jewels, there is little doubt that he signed his own death warrant.[105]

This is extremely interesting, because it completes the journey of Bessie's diamond rings. They were first seen on her fingers when the couple was walking around Jefferson together on January 19, 1877. Next, Jennie Simpson, chambermaid at the Brooks House Hotel, saw them on Abe's fingers as he was lying on a sofa in the parlor the evening that he returned without Bessie – January 21, 1877. He apparently left town with them on the train, and then pawned the rings in St. Louis, Missouri at Walker's Pawn Shop on January 25, just four days after Bessie's alleged murder. Evidence was mounting against Abe.

Rothschild must have been getting antsy sitting in jail, watching the prosecution build a case against him, because a

---

[105] "The Missing Link: Damning Testimony Against Abe Rothschild – Bessie Moore's Diamonds Found in a St. Louis Pawn Shop," The *Times-Picayune*, New Orleans, Louisiana, September 24, 1877, p. 4.

plan was hatched for a prison break. A man named E. Ebberstadt was arrested under a charge of conspiracy to assist Abe Rothschild in breaking jail in Jefferson.[106]

Abe also had a brush with a band of vigilantes in October, as reported by the New Orleans *Times-Picayune*:

At Jefferson, Tex., on the night of the 16th, a band of fifty well-armed and disguised men rode silently into Jefferson, and quietly proceeded to the jail, which they succeeded, without much trouble, in entering. Within its walls were Jim Johnson, the negro who is accused of having murdered Frank Jennings, the mail-rider, and Abe Rothschild, the wealthy young Jew of Cincinnati, who so brutally murdered his mistress, Miss Moore, alias "Diamond Bessie," and is moving heaven and earth, by the aid of his father's money, to escape the just penalty of his crime. After Johnson had been secured by the raiders, their leader, who was evidently a man of culture and great authority, addressed Rothschild in cold and formal tones. He informed the prisoner that in his case they intended to let the law take its course, but if it was shown by the evidence at the trial that there was any likelihood of the ends of justice being thwarted they intended to take him out and hang him like a dog. Rothschild, who, it will be remembered, attempted suicide just previous to his arrest, exhibited the most abject fear at the prospect of death at the hands of the mob. He pleaded piteously for his life, crying bitterly, and was not molested. After the warning an order was given by the leader, and his men quietly filed out of the jail, taking Johnson with them. He was undoubtedly lynched, but his body has not yet been found, nor has any clue as to the identity of any of the raiders been obtained.[107]

---

[106] "Texas," The *Times-Picayune*, New Orleans, Louisiana, November 11, 1877, p. 5.

[107] "Lynch Law" The Chicago *Daily Tribune*, Chicago, Illinois, October 19, 1877, p. 2.

This is very reminiscent of the Stockade Case which took place in Jefferson a decade before, where a band of masked men invaded the jail in Jefferson to murder several people being held there.

A completely different and interesting chapter in the saga of Abe Rothschild comes from the family of William Jefferson (W.J.) Fergusson, who was the Marion County jailer while Rothschild was incarcerated. Fergusson was a witness for the prosecution who testified that Isabella Gouldy had visited Rothschild in his jail cell a few days after he was brought there.

According to accounts handed down in the family, W.J. was responsible for the prisoner, so when a local townsperson baked a Christmas goose for Abe, W.J. had to take a knife and cut the bird apart to make sure no contraband was hidden inside. As the story goes, when W.J. presented the bird to Rothschild, he did so with an apology for having to carve it up first.

W.J. would sometimes bring his five-year-old son John with him to the jail, and the boy and Rothschild became friends. Abe is said to have taught the boy to play cards during his time with him. On July 8, 1877, tragedy struck the Fergusson family. W.J. and his wife Augusta's five-year-old son, John, died.

Abe was apparently saddened over the death of the child, and he wrote a poem of condolence for his jailer. Lee Fergusson, daughter of W.J. Fergusson kept the poem in her Bible and told friends that it was written by Abe Rothschild while he was in jail in Jefferson, guarded by her father.

The poem has been transcribed by Jimmie Fay Chatham, great-granddaughter of W.J. and Augusta Catherine Fergusson, from a copy of a poem in the Fergusson family Bible given to Martha Castleberry Freeman and Joy Tubbs Luttrell, granddaughters of Effie Lee Fergusson Padgett, by her grandmother.

The poem reads as follows:

Dear little Buddie,
Has been called away.
We shall never see him anymore;
His bright little smile
Will ne'er greet us the while,
For he has gone to the other shore.

The dear little boy,
That was his Mother's joy,
Has been by the Reaper claimed;
But we must submit,
To Him who has seen fit,
For it to be so, He has ordained.

His Mother's love, his father's pride
He was with us but a little while;
He is now happy with the angels,
There he waits with a smile.[108]

---

[108] Courtesy of the descendants of William Jefferson Fergusson.

The Continuing Trial in Marshall

The case of the State of Texas vs. Abe Rothschild, charged with the murder of Bessie Moore, was called at 2 p.m. on December 17, 1877.[109]

Speculation about the trial was rampant. The Galveston *Daily News* even reported, "Mr. Gabrielski, a merchant of Overton, is in the city, and brings the information that he has it from counsel for defense that the girl said to have been murdered by Abe Rothschild will be produced alive in court at the trial which begins this week in Jefferson."[110]

When the trial started, the defense petitioned the court to rule that only the State's Prosecutor could continue against Rothschild, on the grounds that neither the State nor individuals could legally employ counsel to prosecute the

[109] "Abe Rothschild: His Case Called Yesterday, and Postponed Till To-Day," The Cincinnati *Enquirer*, Cincinnati, Ohio, December 18, 1877, p. 5.

[110] "Local Personals," The Galveston *Daily News*, Galveston, Texas, December 18, 1877, p. 4.

defendant; that only the State's Attorney, duly elected and qualified, could do so. This was overruled, but it became clear that the tactic of the defense was to get a ruling on every legal proposition that was brought up, and take exception to every ruling of the court so that it could possibly be used on appeal if need be.[111]

Arguments continued on both sides, but on January 2 the Cincinnati *Enquirer* reported that the judge had granted a continuance, which was a postponement of the trial.

Over three months later, the murder case was set for trial on May 7, 1878.[112]

The case was opened with the counsel for Rothschild using a tactic that they had before, asking that the judge to set aside the *venire facias*, or jury pool, of sixty men, citing technicalities in the way that they were called. When the judge held the jury pool to be good, the defendant's counsel asked for a continuance due to prejudice against the prisoner, newspaper articles injurious to him, and that he could not get a fair trial in the county. The judge denied the continuance.[113]

On May 9, the Defendant filed a change of venue request, for the reasons stated above, which the Court agreed to entertain. The Defense Counsel then began to parade witness after witness before the court to show the amount of prejudice that existed in the case. After a number of days, the Court asked just how many witnesses the Defense planned on

---

[111] "Abe Rothschild: Opening of the Trial – His Attorneys Fighting the Case at Every Step," The Cincinnati *Enquirer*, Cincinnati, Ohio, December 19, 1877, p. 4.

[112] "Abe Rothschild's Case Set for May 7," The Galveston *Daily News*, Galveston, Texas, April 23, 1878, p. 1.

[113] "Abe Rothschild – Motion for a Continuance of His Trial Overruled," The Cincinnati *Enquirer*, Cincinnati, Ohio, May 9, 1878, p. 1.

bringing, to which counsel replied that they would call every man in the county until the Court was satisfied.[114]

Finally, Counsel for both sides came to an agreement that the trial should be transferred to another venue, and both agreed on Cass County. Judge B.T. Estes agreed, but suggested that it go to Harrison County since the City of Marshall there was closer than the City of Linden in Cass.[115]

The "Little Virginia" Courthouse in Marshall, Texas,
where the Rothschild trial was held.

Some people may have been frustrated by the amount of time that had already passed in the case, as illustrated by a statement in the Dallas *Commercial* newspaper:

[114] Russell, Traylor. *The Diamond Bessie Murder and the Rothschid Trials* (Waco: Texian Press, 1971), p. 77.
[115] Ibid.

The Dallas Commercial must be hitting at Abe Rothschild when it says, "Something more than a year ago a scamp came into the nearest corner of this State to slay his victim, because he apparently regarded Texas as a good place to commit such deeds. We are sorry to say that the proceedings against him thus far have not indicated that he was mistaken."[116]

Apparently the jailers were getting tired of Abe Rothschild as well, as reported in the *Times-Picayune* on May 29, 1878:

The Marshall Herald occasionally mentions Abe Rothschild, the murderer. The tyrant jailer and Mr. Rothschild have recently had some difficulty. The Herald says: It seems that ill-feeling has existed for some time between Rothschild and the Jefferson jailer, and, as alleged, Rothschild became violent. To make matters worse, Rothschild had, by some means, become possessed of a pocketknife. The jailer sent in a negro to iron the prisoner. A fight ensued, but Rothschild was finally overpowered and ironed. He bit the negro, and the negro bit him on the nose. Rothschild is not seriously hurt, and seems as cheerful as if nothing had happened.[117]

Shortly thereafter, Rothschild was transferred from Jefferson to the jail in Marshall, Texas. His cellmate for at least part of the time was James Currie, a railroad officer, who was charged with the murder of Benjamin C. Porter and the wounding of Maurice Barrymore, both actors, at the railroad station in Marshall on March 19, 1879. Currie is said to have been considered a man of good conduct, but under the influence of alcohol, became enraged and committed the crimes.[118]

---

[116] "Southern States News: Texas," The *Times-Picayune*, New Orleans, Louisiana, May 23, 1878, p. 2.

[117] Ibid.

[118] Russell, Traylor. *The Diamond Bessie Murder and the Rothschid Trials* (Waco: Texian Press, 1971), p. 81.

Cellmates: James Currie, left, and Abe Rothschild, right. (courtesy the Jesse Allen Wise Garden Club)

Abe Rothschild remained in jail in Marshall for some time; as the Times-Picayune newspaper reported, "The case of Abe Rothschild, charged with murder, has been continued for some months on account of absent witnesses."[119]

Finally, on December 17, at 9 a.m., the Court resumed the hearing of the Rothschild murder trial. Witnesses, lawyers, and curious spectators crowded the courtroom.[120]

Judge A.J. Booty presided over the trial, starting with the jury selection, which proved to be quite difficult. It was hard to find a man who did not know of the case, and had not already formed an opinion one way or another. One prospective juror, Jim Durkee, was asked if he had any thoughts on the case. He

---

[119] "Southern States News: Texas," The *Times-Picayune*, New Orleans, Louisiana, June 25, 1878, p. 8.

[120] "Underway – The Trial of Abe Rothschild for Murder," The Cincinnati *Enquirer*, Cincinnati, Ohio, December 18, 1878, p. 2.

replied, "I have. I would hang him." Mr. Durkee was excused from service. Another man, William Sanders, was asked if he had any preconceived notion as to the guilt or innocence of the defendant. He said that he had already formed an opinion, and it would take evidence to change it. The State accepted him, and the Defense Counsel, having exhausted the peremptory challenges, had no choice but to do the same. The final roster of jurors was: R. Vanderslice, Albert Everett, M.T. Preston, W.G. Rudd, C.R. Weathersby, L.M. Fisher, R.A. Shirley, J.C. Lanoue, W.A. Spann, James Summerlin, H.J. Long, and William Sanders.[121]

When the trial began, C.H. Pepper, one of the former proprietors of the Capitol Hotel in Marshall, testified that on Wednesday, January 15, 1877, "A. Rothschild and wife, Cincinnati, Ohio," registered at the hotel as man and wife, and occupied the same room until they took the train to Jefferson.[122]

Dr. Turner of the Brooks House in Jefferson took the stand and testified that Rothschild and the murdered woman had registered as husband and wife on January 19. He also noted that at approximately 11 a.m. on the 21st the defendant and his wife had crossed the bayou on the south side of Jefferson together, and that Rothschild returned alone at about 1 p.m. When questioned about his wife, Abe said that he had left her with friends across the bayou.[123]

A witness named Malloy testified that he saw the deceased and Rothschild cross the bayou bridge together on the 21st,

---

[121] Russell, Traylor. *The Diamond Bessie Murder and the Rothschid Trials* (Waco: Texian Press, 1971), p. 81.
[122] "Underway – The Trial of Abe Rothschild for Murder," The Cincinnati *Enquirer*, Cincinnati, Ohio, December 18, 1878, p. 2.
[123] Ibid.

going in the direction where the woman's body would later be found.[124]

Mr. Spillings, the livery man in Jefferson, took the stand to say that Rothschild had come to his stable on January 21 to hire a horse and buggy to take a lady out riding. Spillings further stated that on February 5 he was called with several others to view the body of the victim.[125]

Several other witnesses testified to much the same series of events. One stated that while the defendant the deceased were in the railroad waiting room in Marshall, preparing to leave for Jefferson, the woman appeared to be in great distress, and was seen shedding tears.[126]

Two witnesses that were missing were Jennie Simpson for the State, the chambermaid at the Brooks House; and Isabella Gouldy for the Defense. There was no explanation for Simpson's absence, and Gouldy had apparently left town to avoid perjury charges.[127]

Even with the testimonies that were presented, the State's case was circumstantial. They could not produce an eyewitness or a "smoking gun." The defense, on the other hand, claimed that Diamond Bessie was seen alive in Jefferson after Rothschild left town, and he therefore could not have murdered her. Also, they asserted that the body could not have been in the woods for sixteen days and been as well-preserved as hers was when discovered.[128]

By December 21 the testimony of the witnesses was complete, and the attorneys began their summations. George

---

[124] "Underway – The Trial of Abe Rothschild for Murder," The Cincinnati *Enquirer*, Cincinnati, Ohio, December 18, 1878, p. 2.

[125] Ibid.

[126] Ibid.

[127] Russell, Traylor. *The Diamond Bessie Murder and the Rothschid Trials* (Waco: Texian Press, 1971), p. 82.

[128] Ibid.

Todd led off for the State in what was termed "an interesting and able argument." Next came Colonel Culberson, who "made a speech that never before had been equaled in Marshall." Following for the Prosecution was Edward Guthridge, and finally Colonel M.L. Crawford, of whom it was said that, "He never wearies a jury with repetition or undue amplification."[129]

Major James Turner then spoke for the Defense for six hours, giving a complete summation of the case. Colonel W.L. Crawford closed for Rothchild's defense, followed by Colonel W.H. Pope who closed for the State. The closing arguments took three full days.[130]

The case was then passed to the jury on December 24, 1878, and their deliberations, which lasted eighteen hours.[131]

It is said that on the foreman C.R. Weathersby drew a hangman's noose on the wall with a pencil, signed his name, and said, "That's my verdict!"[132]

The other jurors reportedly added their names to his, and then wrote their verdict on a piece of paper to return to the court: "We, the jury, find the Defendant Abe Rothschild guilty of murder in the first degree." Rothschild turned pale, but soon got his self-composure.[133]

As he was being led away, Rothschild turned to juror W.G. Rudd, who had once served as a Deputy Sheriff guarding him, and said, "Rudd, you are a hell of a fellow... smoke his cigars, drink his whiskey, and then hang him!" Apparently the Deputy

---

[129] Russell, Traylor. *The Diamond Bessie Murder and the Rothschid Trials* (Waco: Texian Press, 1971), p. 82.

[130] Ibid., p. 83.

[131] "Abe Rothschild of Cincinnati," The *Wyandott Herald*, Kansas City, Kansas, December 26, 1878, p. 2.

[132] Op.cit.. Russell.

[133] Ibid.

had been sharing in some of Rothschild's luxuries provided by his family while serving as his guard.[134]

On December 28, the Marshall Tri-Weekly Herald wrote, "Thus has ended, for the present at least, one of the most important criminal trials in the State of Texas. The general impression among those who heard the evidence is that the verdict is a just one."[135]

Rothschild gave an interview a few days after the verdict, as reported by the *Cincinnati Enquirer* on December 28, 1878:

Abe Rothschild, Interviewed by an Enquirer Reporter
He Declares That He is an Innocent Man

Our Marshall (Texas) correspondent telegraphs us last night as follows:

Your correspondent visited Abe Rothschild this morning. The murderer of Diamond Bessie was found taking a rest in the corridor of the jail, along with the other prisoners. He was walking to and fro vigorously as if to keep himself warm, for the thermometer was sixteen degrees above zero, a very low temperature for this climate. Except a slight degree of nervousness Rothschild's demeanor was as calm and self-possessed as it has been throughout the trial. He shook hands with your correspondent cordially, and cheerfully returned the greeting, "Good morning, Rothschild." When told that the readers of the Globe-Democrat desired to know what he had to say on the subject of his trial, and the crime of which he stood convicted, he replied:

"I am very fond of reading the newspapers, and like to take them, but I do not wish to see them filled with articles at my expense. I would be pleased to unfold to you many things

---

[134] Russell, Traylor. *The Diamond Bessie Murder and the Rothschid Trials* (Waco: Texian Press, 1971), p. 82.
[135] Ibid.

concerning this mystery, but have been advised by my attorneys to be very careful in my interviews with reporters, as I might say something that would go against me in the new hearing I expect to have."

I asked concerning his health and what his feelings were since the verdict of the jury against him. He replied:

"My health is very good under the circumstances, and I feel as cheerful as ever. I eat well, sleep well, and have a clear conscience, having no fears of the result in the end."

"But, Rothschild, are you satisfied you will get a new trial and a reversal of the verdict?"

"Yes, I am confident of it. There are two or three pleas on which I will obtain it – one on account of the non-jurisdiction of this court, from irregular proceedings in the court at Jefferson, on the change of venue, and also on the admissibility of evidence, as it was all circumstantial. Should the motion for a new trial fail, then it will be carried up to the Appellate Court."

"What reason have you to believe that it will not go against you even if you appeal to a higher court?"

"In the first place, I am innocent, and I hope in the end to prove it. This is a great mystery to me, as much so as to any, and it may take a long time to prove my innocence, but in the end I think I will."

"Mr. Rothschild, if you should fail to get a new trial, and your appeal be of no avail, then how stands the matter with you?"

With his right hand on his bosom he said, "I am innocent, and have a clear conscience in the matter. I do not like the idea of being hung, but I am not afraid to die if I just die that way. I die an innocent man, and have no fear of the hereafter."

Your correspondent spent half an hour or more in the prison with Rothschild, and found him a very intelligent man, well posted in the news of the day, and remarkably *communicative. He says he spends at least $100 a year for reading matter, or perhaps more. He is a regular subscriber to several daily papers, and though his cell in every other respect is the same as other prisoners, having only comforts and blankets for a bed, yet a person seeing the newspapers and other literary matter scattered around would suppose him to be the editor-in-chief of one of the first papers of the day. The writer endeavored to draw him out more as to his case, but the above is about all he would say.*

The jurymen who tried this case were all steady farmers but one, and he was a merchant, and the verdict of the jury has given general satisfaction. No one is thirsting for Rothschild's blood, or his neck, but the people generally think the verdict was rendered according to the law and the evidence, and they are satisfied with it.

Your reporter left the prisoner in high spirits, laughing and talking as though no unpleasantness had ever existed between him and Diamond Bessie. He even called the turnkey to testify that he was as cheerful and as happy as ever. [136]

Rothschild obviously had not given up on escaping the charge of murder of Diamond Bessie.

---

[136] "Abe Rothschild, Interviewed by an Enquirer Reporter," The Cincinnati *Enquirer*, Cincinnati, Ohio, December 28, 1878, p. 4.

The Final Trial

On December 30th, 1878, a motion for a new trial was heard by the Court in Marshall. After a six hour debate on the matter between the Defense and the Prosecution, the case was turned over to Judge Booty. He immediately overruled the motion, to which the Defense excepted, and gave notice that they would take their plea to the Court of Appeals. The fact that the District Appellate Court would not be in session until October meant that Abe would spend several more months sitting in jail.[137]

The Austin Weekly Statesman newspaper gave an interesting report on the situation: "The Paris *Banner*, speaking of Abe Rothschild's appeal to the Court of Appeals to get rid of the death sentence given by the Marshall jury, declares that

---

[137] "The Rothschild Case," The *Inter Ocean*, Chicago, Illinois, January 1, 1879, p. 5.

Rothschild will never be hung, but, in less than two years, we shall see him walking free in our streets. Rothschild has too much money to be hung, says the *Banner*."[138]

During his time in jail, Abe certainly had not given up on life. At one point, The *Times-Picayune* reported: "Abe Rothschild, the murderer of Diamond Bessie, has had a glass eye put in his head and a set of false teeth in his mouth."[139]

By November 20, the case was being heard before the Court of Appeals in Tyler, Texas. According to one report it would "probably be decided in a day or two. Both sides seem confident, and especially Rothschild's lawyers, one of whom is Congressman Culberson of East Texas."[140]

In the appeal, the Defense cited thirty-eight formal and eighty general exceptions taken to the ruling of the court, all points on which they felt the conviction should be overturned. These were taken down to six points that were considered in appeal, but in the end, only two proved to be relevant: the first was that the trial court was in error by not exploring an accusation early in the trial by the defense that County Attorney Edward Guthridge was present in the Grand Jury room when a discussion on the indictment was taking place; the second was that juror William Sanders was allowed to serve, even though he expressed under oath during voir dire that he had he already formed an opinion, and it would take evidence to change it.[141]

---

[138] "Texas Facts and Fancies," The Austin *Weekly Statesman*, Austin, Texas, January 9, 1879, p. 2.

[139] "Southern States News: Texas," The *Times-Picayune*, New Orleans, Louisiana, October 21, 1879, p. 4.

[140] "Abe Rothschild's Case," The Cincinnati *Enquirer*, Cincinnati, Ohio, November 20, 1879, p. 4.

[141] "The Rothschild Case," Brenham *Weekly Banner*, Brenham, Texas, January 16, 1880, p. 2.

The evidence of Sanders that was brought before the Court of Appeals is the questioning during his voir dire as follows:

Q. Would we have to introduce evidence to change your opinion, or would you still entertain that opinion and act on it?

A. If the evidence comes in the same as I have heard, of course I would believe it.

Q. What I want to know is this: You say you have an opinion; would you change that opinion if we were to introduce some testimony to show the man was not guilty?

A. Yes sir, I suppose so.

Q. If we did not do that, your opinion is formed conclusively?

A. If the evidence is the same as I have heard it.

Q. Then you have made that option an established opinion?

A. Yes sir.

Q. If it is not, you will change your opinion?

A. Yes sir.

Q. Unless you hear something else, you will maintain the opinion you have?

A. Yes sir.

After which the juror stated, in reply to a question from the court, that if what he had heard was true, then he had a preconceived opinion; but if it was not true, then he should not stand by the opinion. And hearing that, the court overruled the defendant counsel's request for dismissal for cause; because the defendant had exhausted his peremptory challenges, the juror was sworn and took his seat on the jury.[142]

Based on this and other evidence, Judge Clark, of the Court of Appeals, ruled: "The Appellant, stranger though he is,

---

[142] "The Everlasting Rothschild Case," The Austin *Weekly Statesman*, Austin, Texas, January 22, 1880, p. 2.

and guilty though he may be, he has not had a fair and impartial trial."[143]

The Inter Ocean newspaper in Chicago, Illinois reported, "January 14 – The Court of Appeals today reversed and remanded, upon a technicality, the case of Abe Rothschild, charged with the murder of Bessie Moore, near Jefferson, in1877. He has been convicted of murder in the first degree and sentenced to be hanged."[144]

Other newspapers expressed outrage at Judge Clark's opinion, and took it out on the Texas legal system. Editor Charles DeMorse, of the *Northern Standard* at Clarksville, Texas, wrote:

The administration of the criminal law in this state, except as against the poor in purse, is so near a farce that the late decision of the Court of Appeals granting a new trial to Abe Rothschild astonishes no one. We do not say just where the fault lies, but the Court is more interested in preserving some minor technicality than in rendering justice. Certainly all that is required to save a red-handed murderer from the gallows are two or three active friends and sufficient money to employ counsel of experience and ability.[145]

The Galveston Daily News summarized the feelings felt in the State: "The reason given for granting a new trial to Rothschild was that one of the jurors had formed and expressed an opinion in the case previous to the trial. Such a reason seems unreasonable. We don't believe there is an intelligent man in northeast Texas who has not expressed an opinion in the case, and, according to the ruling of the court, the jury must be the veriest set of fools to be found, otherwise they will be

---

[143] Russell, Traylor. *The Diamond Bessie Murder and the Rothschid Trials* (Waco: Texian Press, 1971), p. 84.

[144] "Abe Rothschild," The *Inter Ocean*, Chicago, Illinois, January 15, 1880, p. 5.

[145] Op.cit., p. 85.

disqualified. Better send to the lunatic asylum for a jury and be done with it."[146]

Perhaps The Cincinnati *Enquirer* said it most eloquently: "The case was reversed and remanded; the Court of Appeals had no legal alternative, suffer as the State must from it. But for these inexcusable irregularities, in all probability Abe Rothschild would have been denied further consideration by the Courts, and swung in what atonement his forfeited life could offer for the dastardly crime which stains crimson the fair name of Texas."[147]

By the second week in May, the Defense and Prosecution had agreed that the trial to be set for June 7, 1880. The Milan *Exchange* newspaper reported this, and added the observation, "It is thought that it will be difficult, if not impossible, to obtain twelve intelligent qualified jurors in Harrison County, owing to the public notoriety the case has gained through the press and at the former trial."[148]

It was generally believed that the trial itself would not take place in the current term of court, but instead that only questions of law arising from the Appellate Court decision would be addressed. If this was going to be the case, it would mean that Abe Rothschild would spend more time in a jail cell, biding his time and waiting for a final decision.[149]

Rothschild may have feeling the burdens of his confinement, however, because on July 8 he was part of a plot to escape the jail, as reported by the Dallas *Daily Herald*:

---

[146] The Galveston *Daily News*, Galveston, Texas, Vol. 38, No. 278, February 10, 1880, p. 2.

[147] "Texas Justice: Abe Rothschild's Escape From a Deserved Hanging," The Cincinnati *Enquirer*, Cincinnati, Ohio, January 25, 1880, p. 8.

[148] "Southern Gleanings," The Milan *Exchange*, Milan, Tennessee, May 13, 1880, p. 6.

[149] "Abe Rothschild to Be Called to an Account on the 7th," The Cincinnati *Enquirer*, Cincinnati, Ohio, May 31, 1880, p. 4.

Abe Rothschild and his Cell Mate in Irons

Abe Rothschild, the murderer of "Diamond" Bessie Moore, and E.J. Manus, a horse-thief, confined in the same cell, are both in chains for attempting to escape today by sawing the bars. Henry Moore, the negro boy who conveyed the saw, knife and file to the prisoners, was arrested and jailed by Sheriff Perry today.[150]

Henry Moore was only seventeen years old, and confessed to Sheriff Perry that Rothschild was going to pay him $50 for the job. He further said that Manus was going to do the work and then lead Abe to a place of safety, and Rothschild was going to foot the bill for the entire operation.[151]

As Rothschild sat in jail, the time until his trial dragged on. A date was finally set for November 24, 1880.[152] When the trial arrived it was discovered that the indictment against the defendant was missing. This caused an automatic continuance until the indictment could be found, or a substitute filed.[153]

Rothschild's case came up for trial again on November 26 in Marshall before Judge Booty. The defense· asked for a continuance once again, which was overruled. Counsel for the defense then moved to quash the indictment against Rothschild for the reasons for which the Court of Appeals reversed the first decision. The first was the claim that Edward Guthridge, County Attorney of Marion County when the indictment was being discussed and voted on, was in the grand jury room. Two of the grand jurymen swore positively that he was not present,

---

[150] "Abe Rothschild and his Cell Mate in Irons," The Dallas *Daily Herald*, Dallas, Texas, July 9, 1880, p. 1.

[151] "Attempted Escape of Abe Rothschild," The *Times-Picayune*, New Orleans, Louisiana, July 12, 1880, p. 4.

[152] "Abe Rothschild's Case," The Cincinnati *Enquirer*, Cincinnati, Ohio, October 30, 1880, p. 5.

[153] "Peculiar Practice in Abe Rothschild's Case," The Cincinnati *Enquirer*, Cincinnati, Ohio, November 25, 1880, p. 1.

which was backed up by the written deposition of Guthridge himself. On the other hand, two other witnesses swore that he was present in the grand jury room. The conflicting testimony, and the fact that the court where he was found guilty did not investigate the claim, was problematic.[154]

Based on that, and the allowing of juror William Sanders without contestation, on November 29, Judge Booty sustained the defendant's motion to set aside the indictment.[155] The question remained, however, of where any new proceedings would take place. Since the crime was committed in Marion County, that is where any new action would have to originate. While this was being decided Rothschild was taken back to jail, where he had served approximately three years and eight months – at a cost of at least $10,000 to Marion and Harrison Counties, and the State of Texas.[156]

An affidavit was once again made at Jefferson on December 1, again charging Rothschild with murder. A warrant was issued for his arrest, which was carried out at the Harrison County jail. Abe was returned to the Jefferson jail, and the grand jury that was in session issued an indictment for murder in the first degree. The court ordered the bill filed and the case was scheduled for trial in December. A venire of sixty potential jurors was drawn in the hopes that twelve could be selected.[157]

Judge B.T. Estes of Jefferson announced that the case would once and for all be tried, showing his determination to

[154] "The Rothschild Case," The *Times-Picayune*, New Orleans, Louisiana, December 6, 1880, p. 3.

[155] "The Judge of the Court Rules in Favor of Abe Rothschild, The Murderer, and Probably Renders His Trial Impossible," The *Times-Picayune*, New Orleans, Louisiana, December 1, 1880, p. 1.

[156] "The Rothschild Case," The *Times-Picayune*, New Orleans, Louisiana, December 6, 1880, p. 3.

[157] "Affidavit was Made," The Brenham *Weekly Banner*, Brenham, Texas, December 9, 1880, p. 1.

bring an end to the Rothschild affair that had dragged on for so long.[158]

The jury was ordered to appear on December 14, and the actual start of the trial was delayed until the 16th. At time a motion was immediately filed by the defense counsel to quash the indictment on the grounds that: 1) the offense was not charged in plain and intelligible language; 2) it charged two separate offenses, and 3) the allegations of the indictment were inconsistent, repugnant, and contradictory. Judge B.T. Estes overruled the motion.[159]

The defense counsel then moved for a continuance based on the absence of four key witnesses: Isabella Gouldy, A.J. Stambaugh, A.P. Brown, and Peter Smith. Isabella Gouldy was set to testify that she saw Diamond Bessie on January 20, 1877 in Jefferson, and again on Thursday after the Sunday she was supposed to have been murdered. On that Thursday Bessie was supposedly on the south side of the bayou in the company of a man other than the defendant. Isabella saw Bessie stop; she seemed to be pinning her garter and adjusting her stocking. When Bessie's dead body was found, Isabella Gouldy was one of the ladies charged with undressing the corpse and dressing it in burial clothes. At that time she reportedly recognized Bessie as the woman that she had seen with the man on the south side of the bayou, and also noticed that one of her garters was pinned to the stocking.[160] The defense further stated that A.J. Stambaugh would testify that he saw Bessie Moore alive on Polk St. in Jefferson ten days prior to February 5, 1877, after Rothschild had left by train.[161]

---

[158] Russell, Traylor. *The Diamond Bessie Murder and the Rothschid Trials* (Waco: Texian Press, 1971), p. 93.
[159] Ibid.
[160] Ibid.
[161] Ibid.

As to the missing witness A.P. Brown, defense counsel claimed that he was a medical doctor who saw the body soon after it was found. Brown would testify that due to the lack of decomposition, there was no way that the woman could have been dead from January 21 to February 5.[162]

Finally, the witness Peter Smith, if present, would testify that as an employee of the Brooks House, he waited on Rothschild at supper the Sunday of the supposed murder, and the Defendant was not wearing any rings or other jewelry. Furthermore, he would explain that Jennie Simpson, a witness for the prosecution, lived in a house in the yard of the Brooks House and was far removed from the Defendant's room and therefore could not have heard anything from the Rothschild room that she testified about.[163]

In response to the Defense's motion for continuance, the State argued that Isabella Gouldy had been a fugitive from justice for over two years, having fled town after a perjury charge arising from her testimony at the Habeas Corpus hearing in 1877, and that the other witnesses were in either Harrison or Marion counties, and available for trial. Judge B.T. Estes overruled the motion.[164]

On December 17, Rothschild was arraigned and pleaded not guilty to the charges. A jury was seated, and consisted of: J.S. Page, J.T. Smith, W.H. Green, George W. Woods, Aaron Jackson, Adam Stoll, D.S. Smith, W.N. Jaques, G.W. Watson, George W. Jackson, W.F. Jackson, and Archie Adams. Two of the jurors, D.S. Smith and Archie Adams, were black men. This was very unusual because it was so close to the Civil War and reconstruction, and black men were not usually allowed to serve on juries. During the trial the jury stayed at the Excelsior

---

[162] Russell, Traylor. *The Diamond Bessie Murder and the Rothschid Trials* (Waco: Texian Press, 1971), p. 94.
[163] Ibid.
[164] Ibid.

House, and registered every night under the name "Jury in Rothschild Case." After the names of D.S. Smith and Archie Adams is the notation "(col.)."[165]

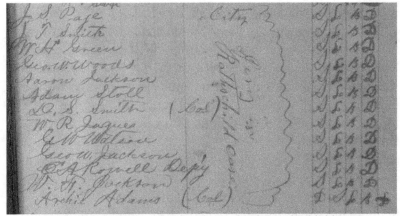

The Excelsior House Hotel register with the Rothschild jurors

The presentation of witnesses began on December 22 to a packed courtroom, including reporters from Jefferson, Marshall, Shreveport, Dallas, Cincinnati, and other cities as well.[166]

The trial was in full swing on December 24, and The Cincinnati *Enquirer* reported:

Nothing new of special importance in Abe Rothschild's case was developed today. Six more witnesses have been examined for the State, the evidence generally being about the same as that at the first trial, except that some of the colored witnesses have forgotten some things. The trial will not close before the middle of next week, and the Court and jury will miss their Christmas. There were but few people about the

---

[165] Russell, Traylor. *The Diamond Bessie Murder and the Rothschid Trials* (Waco: Texian Press, 1971), p. 94.
[166] Ibid.

Courthouse today, and interest in the case seems to be losing ground.[167]

A few days later, the Cincinnati *Enquirer* wrote:

"At the opening of the court at nine o'clock this morning it was announced that District Attorney C.S. Todd was sick, and the court appointed George T. Todd, Esq., to represent him.

"The evidence on the part of the defense was closed early this evening, after which the State introduced several new witnesses, principally in regard to the state of the weather during the time the murdered woman was supposed to have been exposed.

"The evidence differed very materially, as it was only from recollection that the witnesses could give their opinion. It was proven by one of the State's witnesses that the body of a prominent citizen who died during the trial had decomposed inside of twenty-four hours. One witness stated that he was at or near the spot where the body was found on the 28th of January, and that he did not see it at that time. The evidence has closed, and argument will begin at eight o'clock tomorrow morning. It will probably take ten days for the speeches on both sides."[168]

On December 27, 1880, both sides had exhausted their presentations, and therefore rested. Judge B.T. Estes read the charge to the jury, pointing out that the State's case was one of circumstantial evidence, and in each case of circumstance the Defendant's guilt has to be clearly and distinctly proven. He charged the jury that, for a verdict of guilty, "The whole of the

---

[167] "Abe Rothschild's Case," The Cincinnati *Enquirer*, Cincinnati, Ohio, December 24, 1880, p. 1.

[168] "Abe Rothschild: All the Testimony in and Argument of His Case to Begin Today," The Cincinnati Enquirer, Cincinnati, Ohio, December 28, 1880, p. 4.

testimony must be sufficient to exclude every other hypotheses than that of the guilt of the Defendant."[169]

If the verdict that was returned was one of guilt, the punishment would be either death or life imprisonment. After closing arguments from both sides, on December 28, Judge B.T. Estes instructed the members of the jury, "Gentlemen, you will retire and consider your verdict."[170]

The town of Jefferson was buzzing with talk of the impending verdict, and men in the saloons of the city were betting wildly. At 8 p.m. that evening, the bailiff heard a knock on the inside of the jury room door. When he opened it, he spoke with the foreman of the jury, then returned to the courtroom to tell the judge that a verdict had been reached. The jury was returned, and Judge B.T. Estes cautioned the crowd against any outcry or demonstration. He further had the sheriff clear the aisles and hallways. The foreman of the jury handed the written verdict to the bailiff, who passed it to the Court Clerk. Judge B.T. Estes said, "Mr. Clerk, you will read the verdict."[171]

The clerk opened the paper, and read, "We, the jury, find the Defendant Abe Rothschild not guilty. – John T. Smith, Foreman."[172]

There was silence for a moment, and the courtroom erupted. The next morning, the *Times-Picayune* newspaper reported:

When the verdict of "not guilty" in the case of Abe Rothschild, for the murder of Bessie Moore, was read, the excitement in the courtroom was so intense that it was with

---

[169] Russell, Traylor. *The Diamond Bessie Murder and the Rothschid Trials* (Waco: Texian Press, 1971), p. 98.
[170] Ibid.
[171] Russell, Traylor. *The Diamond Bessie Murder and the Rothschid Trials* (Waco: Texian Press, 1971), p. 99.
[172] Ibid.

difficulty that order was restored. Rothschild left for Cincinnati this morning. The theory of his attorney was that Bessie Moore committed suicide, and that the body could not remain exposed for almost fifteen days without showing more signs of decomposition.[173]

The Chicago *Daily Tribune* reported, *"Jefferson, Tex., Dec. 30. – Abe Rothschild, who murdered his mistress some three years ago, and whose case has attracted a good deal of attention in different parts of the country, was acquitted here today."*[174]

Rothschild's defense is said to have cost $40,000.[175] In today's dollar value, that is approximately $1,000,000.

Few people seemed surprised at the acquittal in the trial. Mr. Rothschild, Abe's father, told the Cincinnati *Enquirer* that he was thinking about starting a business somewhere in the South, perhaps even in Texas. Mr. Rothschild speculated that the case would be a great asset to the business.[176]

Some newspapers were less than kind when talking about the verdict, however. The Galveston Daily News said, "The Advocate says of the acquittal of Abe Rothschild: 'The verdict is a disgrace to any jury of any land.'"[177]

The Fort Wayne *Daily Gazette* quoted the Austin *Dispatch*, saying: "The acquittal of Abe Rothschild, charged with the murder of Bessie Moore, is another dark blot on Texas. The Dispatch declares it was a most cold-blooded

---

[173] "A Batch of Texas News Products," The *Times-Picayune*, New Orleans, Louisiana, January 1, 1881, p. 8.

[174] "Acquitted," The Chicago *Daily Tribune*, Chicago, Illinois, December 31, 1880, p. 5.

[175] "The Defense of Abe Rothschild," The *Inter Ocean*, Chicago, Illinois, January 1, 1881, p. 1.

[176] "Utilizing Abe's Little Adventure as an Advertisement," The Cincinnati *Enquirer*, Cincinnati, Ohio, January 5, 1881, p. 4.

[177] "State Press," The Galveston *Daily News*, Galveston, Texas, January 6, 1881, p. 2.

atrocity. Rothschild married Bessie at Danville, Illinois, and then brought her to Texas for the express purpose of murdering her for her diamonds. It adds that the verdict in the case is an invitation to every man, in the north, who desires to get rid of someone who is in his way, to lure his victim to Texas and if he has the means to employ able lawyers, he may murder him (or her) with impunity. This is pretty plain, plucky talk – and a few years ago would have cost the editor his scalp."[178]

Only a few days after the acquittal, advertisements began to appear for an illustrated book on the entire story of the Diamond Bessie affair. Apparently the case was big enough that someone was compiling the story as it developed, and once it was done, the advertisement claimed that it was the "fastest selling book in the world!" While that certainly can't be proven, ads for the book ran in papers across the county. The following advertisement ran in the Dallas *Daily Herald* newspaper on January 19, 1881, p. 5:

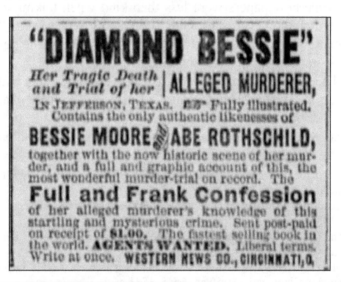

[178] "The Acquittal of Abe Rothschild," Fort Wayne *Gazette*, Fort Wayne, Indiana, January 14, 1881, p. 2.

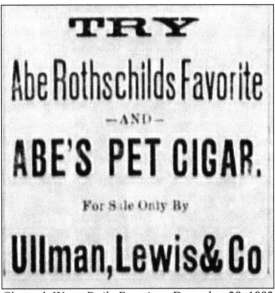

Cigar ad, Waco *Daily Examiner*, December 28, 1882

Rothschild After the Trials

Instead of simply fading away after so much time in jail and the notoriety involved, Abe Rothschild continued to make headlines... and even got an endorsement or two, as witnessed by the ad above.

Some people believe that he was set to capitalize on his notoriety – for example, the Houston *Post* remarks that "Abe Rothschild has not yet started out on a lecturing tour."[179]

But perhaps that was simply tongue in cheek, because less than a year after the trial, Abe Rothschild was back in the business of being a travelling salesman, or drummer as they were known in the day. The Fort Wayne *Daily Gazette*

[179] "Editorial Notes," Brenham *Weekly Banner*, Brenham, Texas, January 13, 1881, p. 1.

reported on April 28, 1881, "Abe Rothschild, a Cincinnati drummer, is in the city. He will be remembered as having long suffered imprisonment in Texas for the alleged murder of "Diamond Bessie" Moore, a notorious female of Chicago.[180]

Rothschild was recognized wherever he went, as shown in an article from the Sedalia, Missouri newspaper in August of 1881:

"A noted murderer was in the city this morning and took whisky straight at the Garrison house bar. It was none other than Abe Rothschild, of Cincinnati, Ohio, who laid in jail at Marshall, Texas nearly four years, for the murder of his mistress, 'Diamond Bessie.' Rothschild's father expended a fortune in defense of his son, and his effort was rewarded at last by a jury bringing in a verdict of acquittal. It was one of the most cold blooded murders in the annals of crime, and if Rothschild had received his dues, he would now be in a climate where it is much warmer than it was in Sedalia during the past week. He left for Lexington on Conductor Marsh's train this morning."[181]

On October 28, 1881, a reporter from the Denver *Colorado Republican* newspaper caught up with the acquitted murderer as he was about to leave town. The reporter interviewed him and wrote the following story:

Abe Rothschild, The Alleged Murderer of "Diamond Bessie," Explains How He Cheated the Hangman

A Republican reporter yesterday morning met Abe Rothschild at the Union Depot just as he was ready to take the Union Pacific train for the east. The notoriety which

---

[180] "Amusements," Fort Wayne *Daily Gazette*, Fort Wayne, Indiana, April 28, 1881, p. 5.

[181] "A Noted Murderer at the Garrison," The Sedalia *Weekly Bazoo*, Sedalia, Missouri, August 23, 1881, p. 6.

Rothschild acquired in connection with the murder of "Diamond Bessie" Moore in Texas led the reporter to seek an interview, the result of which will be found below:

The murder of "Diamond Bessie" and Abe Rothschild's subsequent arrest in Cincinnati formed one of the greatest sensations in the criminal annals of that city. The first intimation of the murder obtained at Cincinnati was supplied by a circular to the chief of police, announcing that the mutilated body of a woman had been found in the woods near Marshall, Texas. She had been seen in the company with an unknown man, who took her out in a buggy and returned without her, saying he had left her with some friends. When the body was discovered the jewelry had all been removed, and one of the fingers had been severed to take off a diamond ring, after which the body had been concealed under rocks and rubbish. The man who was with her had evidently registered under an assumed name, as he could not be traced back.

About a week after the Cincinnati police received this circular, a mysterious shooting occurred; very late one night, at Jake Ogg's club-house in that city, the victim being a prominent young fellow of the town, named Abe Rothschild.

The ball had entered his head near the eye and produced a ghastly wound. He volunteered the statement that he had shot himself accidentally and was removed to his father's house. That day another circular was received from Texas, saying that by means of scrutinizing the handwritings on various Texas registers, the detectives had become convinced that the man who was with "Diamond Bessie" was one Abe Rothschild, whose handwriting resembled that of the mysterious lover. A guard was immediately stationed at Rothschild's bed-room, and when he recovered he was taken to jail, and afterward, by a detective's trick, was conveyed, in the face of a habeas corpus proceeding, to Texas. He lay in prison three years, when his release followed.

When the Republican reporter met him at the depot yesterday morning his appearance was peculiar. He was about five feet, ten inches high, of a stout build. He is not obese, but his physique denotes considerable muscular power. His neck, set between two strong shoulders, is thick, and widens in front, as it rises to a full, round face, though the proportions of the face are not formed from flabby fat. He has black hair and brown eyes. The eyes are the most striking feature to an observer at the first glance. They are large, protruding and very round, with scarcely any perceptible elongation. His head is large and round, and his nose indicates a decidedly aggressive possessor. The vomer appears abnormally large and the nostrils dilated, and the structure is crowned by a decisive pug. He has a thin, short, silken mustache. His dress was that of an ordinary traveling businessman. A narrow-rolled brim slouch hat, a sack coat of the texture denominated pepper and salt, and vest and pantaloons of the same kind.

After the usual preliminary greetings, the reporter remarked:

"Mr. Rothschild, on account of the great public interest manifested in the trouble you got into in Texas, we would like to hear your version of that matter."

"Well, I don't care to give you any version of it. I am in business now, and keeping this thing alive does more harm than good."

"What business are you in?"

"Here is my card," and he handed the scribe a card of M. Rothschild & Co., Manufacturers and Importers, etc.

"The papers never contained a very full account of your trial, did they?"

"Well, they all got the same account; there was a six-line associated press dispatch sent out, and I do not care to add any more to it."

"What was your defense, Mr. Rothschild?"

100

"I do not see any good in talking about it, and decline to tell."

"Were you not acquitted?"

"Oh, yes. The jury was out only one hour and fifteen minutes before they agreed. But most of that time was occupied by them in eating supper. You know how it is with a country jury; they must have their regular rations."

"It seems then, that you had a complete defense?"

"I would think so. Why, I proved an alibi."

"But was not that evidence contested by Texas witnesses?"

"Not positively. Well, I see I may as well tell you. My defense rested on two grounds. One was the alibi; the other was a failure of the proof to sustain the indictment. You know the prosecution must charge in the indictment the crime and the day when it was committed. This indictment did so, but it stated that the day on which the murder was committed was a certain one, and the evidence showed that the body was found twenty-five days after the day so alleged, and the proof was that when it was found there were no signs of decomposition. Then medical experts were called who proved that it was impossible for a body to lie in a position exposed to the Texas weather so long without becoming badly decayed. And I also proved conclusively that I was not in Texas on the day the murder was committed, as alleged in the indictment."

"Was the trial a very exciting one?"

"Very much so. It lasted five weeks. I was acquitted last December."

"What attorneys did you have?"

"Oh, they were all local attorneys; all living in Marshall, where I was tried."

"What do you think of Texas?"

"I have nothing to say against it. Of course, I did not see much of it, so I cannot form a very correct opinion."

"You have been in Denver before?" was asked.

"Quite often. I am selling goods here. I will be back in six weeks again. Here is the bill I sold this trip." and he showed a schedule of orders obtained from some of Denver's prominent merchants. The reporter asked Mr. Rothschild what he thought of Colorado. "I am infatuated with it," he replied; "I think it is the best place and Denver leads, for its size, any place I ever saw."

After the statement of other unimportant matters which were personal and not for publication, Mr. Rothschild extended a very cordial invitation to his interrogator to call upon him in Cincinnati, if he ever reached that city, and a compliance was promised. Farewells were exchanged and the commercial traveler took his place on the train and was soon whirling along eastward.

A mere three months later, however, Rothschild was back in the news, this time being accused of running a mail-fraud scheme. On January 5, 1882, the Kansas newspaper *Atchinson Globe* wrote:

Abe Rothschild, an ex-murderer of Cincinnati, is under suspicion of being engaged in fraudulent practices, using the United States mails to swindle the unwary. He is a member of a Firm which, it is understood, advertises in religious papers and country weeklies, offering, for the sum of one dollar, to send a certain number of cigarettes and a package of confectionary. The money obtained, nothing is sent, and their advertising bills are not paid. It is a notorious fact that when a man wants to advertise a swindle, he always selects the religious newspaper as his advertising medium. The Kansas Methodist, the organ of the Methodist Church in this state, advertises more swindles than any secular paper we know of. The Methodist may claim that it does not know it is advertising swindles, but we do not believe it. It is now advertising a beautiful revolver, worth six dollars, which will be given as a premium to the subscribers of a certain monthly magazine, price one dollar. This swindle is so apparent that even the editor of a religious paper ought to see it, and doubtless would see it were he not blinded by miserable cupidity.

This episode was to be the first in a long criminal career in which Abe Rothschild employed many aliases, including Henry Smythe, H.T. Jackson, R.L. Miller, J.C. Coleman, T.M. Jones, T. Hutton, and the colorful Diamond Charley.[182]

In 1894, Rothschild (using the name Henry Smythe) had been taken into custody for mail fraud in San Francisco by U.S. Marshall Henry Maier. The marshal was bringing the suspect back east by train to stand trial, when he prepared coffee for himself and the prisoner. An hour and a half later, the lawman woke up with a drowsy feeling and a terrible headache, only to find that Rothschild had escaped when the train stopped in Little Rock, Arkansas, to take on water. The officer was certain that Rothschild had slipped some kind of drug into the coffee.[183]

The near-capture didn't slow Rothschild down; a year later he is reported to have swindled Atlanta, Georgia jewelers out of $3,000 worth of merchandise. His game was well thought out and executed. First, he took lodging at the Rountree House in Swainsboro, Georgia under the name "J.C. Coleman," a name that he most likely found in the Bradstreet Business Listing which rated the credit of merchants. Coleman had a credit rating of $175,000, which was an astronomical sum in those days and the most likely reason Rothschild chose his name. To further establish himself, he rented a building in town and spread the word that he was opening a jewelry store. Using an official letterhead that he'd printed, "Coleman" then wrote

---

[182] "Coleman Has Another Alias," The Atlanta *Constitution*, Atlanta, Georgia, March 30, 1895.

[183] "The Coffee Was Drugged," The Ogden Utah *Standard*, Ogden, Utah, November 14, 1894.

to a number of Atlanta jewelers requesting diamond rings, watches, and other precious items to be used as stock in his new store. When the jewelers, who were unaware how many of their associates had also been contacted, checked J.C. Coleman's Bradstreet credit rating, they found it to be excellent. The merchandise was shipped immediately, only to be received by Rothschild, who then fled the city.[184]

The description of Rothschild was published in The Atlanta *Constitution*: *He is a very large man, weighing 200 pounds. He has a full face, dark peculiar eyes. The right eye is glassy. His hair is black. He wore a derby hat and Prince Albert coat.*[185]

Rothschild was so successful with this con that The Atlanta *Constitution* next reported: *It was learned yesterday that Atlanta had not suffered alone. Macon, Augusta, Charleston and Savannah merchants are all reported to have fallen victims to the huge swindle. It was an elaborate fraud, planned, perfected and systematized by astute and experienced professionals. The extent of the steal is not known but it is supposed to amount to $10,000.*[186]

His crimes were so serious that over 10,000 flyers with his description and crimes were distributed throughout the nation, and beyond. Ten days later, an arrest was made in Canada of T. Hutton, a.k.a. J.C. Coleman, a.k.a. Diamond Charley, a.k.a. Abe Rothschild.[187]

On March 28, 1895, Rothschild was carried before a magistrate in Toronto, where he was remanded to jail without

---

[184] "Big Diamond Robbery Played by a Bold Crook on Atlanta Merchants," The Atlanta *Constitution*, Atlanta, Georgia 3/14/1895.

[185] "The News From Swainsboro," The Atlanta *Constitution*. Atlanta, Georgia, 3/14/1895.

[186] "Off With The Gems" The Atlanta *Constitution*, Atlanta, GA. 3/15/1895.

[187] "Caught In Canada: Coleman, Known as Diamond Charley, Arrested and Jailed in Toronto," The Atlanta *Constitution*, Atlanta, Georgia 3/25/1895.

bail. That same day F.J. Dodge, a detective representing the Wells-Fargo Express Company, arrived in Toronto to begin proceedings for the extradition of the prisoner.[188]

The prisoner fought extradition for several months, but on June 19, 1895, The Atlanta *Constitution* reported:

Judge MacDougall this afternoon ordered the extradition of James Hutton, alias "Diamond Charley," the alleged diamond thief who was arrested at St Mary's, Ont., a few months ago, charged with swindling Toronto and Hamilton jewelers. Judge MacDougall granted the extradition on two warrants, one consigning Hutton to Swainsboro, Ga, the other to Moberly, Mo. The prisoner has thirty days in which to appeal.

Nine months later on March 16, 1896, the extradition, trial, and sentencing were over. Rothschild had reached an agreement with the court, and pled guilty to a charge of forgery. By accepting guilt for his use of aliases, he had completely escaped any charge associated with the theft that he had perpetrated. His sentence was four years in the penitentiary.[189]

As more about Rothschild became known, The Atlanta *Constitution* reported:

Rothschild is one of the widest known crooks in the country. His fame is international. Rothschild is wanted in nearly every state in the union. After working several southern states getting away with several thousand dollars, he went to Havana, Cuba. Shortly afterward he was traced to Swainsboro, Ga. , where he worked a jeweler for $4,000. From there he made a circuitous route through several states and finally

---

[188] "Doesn't Want To Come Here: Coleman the Diamond Swindler, is Contented in the Canada Jail," The Atlanta *Constitution*, Atlanta, Georgia, March 29, 1895.

[189] "Four Years for Abe," The Atlanta *Constitution*, Atlanta, Georgia, March 16, 1896.

wound up in St. Mary's, Canada, and when about to work another job there he was arrested.

A more thorough summation of Abe Rothschild's life was printed in The *Evening Times*, Washington, D.C., on July 1, 1897:

Crimes by the Hundred: Abe Rothschild, Swindler by Instinct, Owns Up to a Multitude

A United States post office inspector was discussing crime with a reporter for The Times this morning, and in telling of some of the great and skillful crimes which have been run down by the inspectors' corps, he recalled the case of Abe Rothschild. This man had a long career as a swindler of the gilt-edge type. With it all, he is charged with having been a blackened criminal. Two of his important aliases were Joseph Jaeger and Henry Smyth. He was arrested at San Lorenzo, Cal., September 30, 1894, by an inspector attached to the San Francisco division, for crimes alleged to have been committed in Missouri during the summer of 1894. The charge against him was "using the mails in conducting a scheme to defraud."

One of Rothschild's plans was to learn the name of a business man of high standing in some particular town. Then he would forge an order in the name of this man on some big city dealer, who would ship the goods either to the place at which the man lived or to some place nearby, where, as the swindler stated, he was about to open a "racket store." The goods were nearly always shipped as requested. The swindler would then assume the name of the business man, and have a large quantity of mail addressed to himself at the point to which the goods were to be shipped. Rothschild would reach the place about two days before the goods were due, and by claiming the letters at the post office and by making inquiries at the freight and express offices would establish his identity under the name assumed. He would have no difficulty in getting the goods when they arrived. Then he would disappear. His plunder usually consisted of diamonds, jewelry, or valuable articles of small bulk which he could stow away in his baggage.

Sometimes Rothschild would order the goods sent to the very place at which the real business man lived. He would first inquire at the post office, and when told that the most prominent business man in town also bore the name he mentioned, Rothschild would be astounded, and would call upon the man whose name he had assumed. Rothschild would then receive from this man the letters which he (Rothschild) had caused to be mailed to that name and address. The real business man had been receiving these letters for several days, and had been unable to comprehend them. The arrival of this stranger cleared matters up.

Rothschild had such a complete knowledge of the contents of the letters, that the real business man would not suspect that they had not been intended for the man who had called upon him. In this way he established his identity, and when the goods came by express he would have no trouble in getting possession of them. On March 13, 1894, he secured $4,000 in diamonds in this way at Swainsboro, Ga.

After he had been arrested in California, it was agreed to remove him to Missouri, where the offenses for which he was wanted had been committed. The prisoner escaped from the deputy marshal at Little Rock, Ark., on November 12, 1894. After his escape, he operated the same scheme through Mexico, Cuba and through several of the Southern States, and was rearrested at St. Mary's, Ontario, on March 25, 1895, while he was in the act of receipting for express packages. He was extradited and tried at Moberly, Mo., and sentenced to four years' imprisonment. After the expiration of this term he will be taken to Swainsboro, Ga., for trial.

Rothschild is about forty-seven years old. He is the son of a prominent jeweler and banker at Cincinnati. He killed "Diamond Bessie" Moore, a woman of bad repute at Jefferson, Tex. He was arrested at Cincinnati for this crime and attempted to commit suicide, but succeeded only in shooting out one eye. After his recovery, he was taken down to Texas and escaped being lynched by a mere chance. He was convicted and sentenced to be hanged, but the verdict was reversed by the Supreme Court, and, after four years of trouble, he was acquitted.

Rothschild was involved in a business failure in New York City, in which the liabilities were $750,000. He was tried for fraud, but acquitted. After this he became known as a horseman and gambler in London, Paris, and other European capitals. According to the confession of Rothschild, there are over 200 criminal charges against him in the United States, Mexico, Canada, England, France and Cuba.

In his defense he pleaded that his victims were always wealthy people, express companies, railroad companies and banks. He claimed never to have defrauded a person who was poor.

This alone would be an accomplished lifetime resume for any hardened criminal, but Abe Rothchild's exploits did not stop there. In 1899 he was arrested again for mail fraud, and at that time attempted to bribe the police officers to let him go. He had in his possession a roll of money, but it turned out to be counterfeit. He was arraigned, tried, and once again sentenced to jail time.[190]

During a prisoner transport in 1899 on a train, he was shackled to another con man named Stansfield. Together the two men hatched a plan, and leapt from the moving train to

---

[190] "Bribe Offered to Officers by Abe Rothschild was in Counterfeit Money," The Cincinnati *Enquirer*, Cincinnati, Ohio, Apr 4 1899, p. 12.

freedom. When they asked a blacksmith to break off their manacles, the man refused and quickly alerted the authorities. Rothschild and Stansfield were quickly captured and taken to face more charges. The Fort Wayne *News* observed: *Rothschild is one of the most noted criminals in this country, and his escape was greatly deplored.*[191]

He was returned to prison, but during that time the Wells-Fargo Express Company was pursuing charges against Rothschild in Texas for crimes of fraud committed there. He was tried there, and in July of 1899, convicted and given three years in the penitentiary.[192]

Three years and two months later, Rothschild was out of jail and in trouble with the law once again. On June 17, 1902, he was arrested using the alias of A.M. Graham for running a diamond swindling operation in Shippensburg, Pennsylvania. The arrest was made on a wire dispatch received from Washington, D.C., by local authorities: "Arrest Abe Rothschild, notorious diamond swindler, attempted swindle at Shippensburg and escaped. He is a Jew weighing 240 pounds, black moustache, glass eye, aged 50 years, has long penitentiary record. Arrest and wire." Rothschild was seen leaving the barber shop of a hotel, where he had his moustache shaved off. He was arrested by the police while making inquiries as to the location of the Y.M.C.A. rooms. He had been in Shippensburg since Saturday, having registered at the Temperance Hotel. When his room was searched a loaded .38 caliber revolver was found concealed between the sheets, along with documents pertaining to his con scheme. When he was locked up in the Dauphin county prison, Rothschild said to the

---

[191] "Their Bold Dash: Manacles Bound Two Prisoners Together, and Together They Escaped," The Fort Wayne *News*. Fort Wayne Ind., April 7, 1899.

[192] "Diamond Thief is Sentenced," The Fort Wayne *News*, Fort Wayne, Indiana, July 20, 1899.

arresting officer, "I am the man you want, but you can give Post Office Inspector Sutton some credit for the arrest, however."[193]

Rothschild's trial was held a few months later in September. An accomplice, Thomas B. Best, turned states' evidence and took the stand against Abe.[194]

On September 11, 1902, Abe Rothschild was found guilty of conspiring to defraud thirty leading diamond dealers of a quarter of a million dollars' worth of diamonds by the impersonation of George H. Stewart, a millionaire grain dealer at Shippensburg, and ordering the gems to be sent by express to Shippensburg, where he pretended to open a jewelry store. This was a con that he had run in the past, and had also been previously convicted of in Georgia.[195] He was again sentenced to a term in prison for his crime.[196]

Once released, he apparently continued his criminal career. The last reported incident came in New York, and was reported by the newspaper the New York *Tribune* on March 14, 1908:

Abe Rothschild Again Betrayed by Glass Eye: "Diamond Bessie's" Slayer Caught at Get-Rich-Quick Game Here

When someone complained three days ago to Walter S. Mayer, post office inspector in charge of the New York district, that the man with the glass eye who seemed to be in charge of

---

[193] "Diamond Swindler is Under Arrest," The Scranton *Republican*, Scranton, PA, June 16, 1902.

[194] "Trial of Abe Rothschild Begun at Carlisle, Pa.," *The Jewelers' Circular-Weekly* September 10, 1902.

[195] "Diamond Swindler Guilty," The New York *Times*, New York, NY, September 11, 1902.

[196] Bluefield *Daily Telegraph*, Bluefield, West Virginia, September 17, 1902.

the office of "The Successful Business Man," at No. 302 Broadway, was handling a "con" game to the readers of the spiritedly written circulars advertising that publication-to-be, Mr. Mayer listened attentively.

When he was reminded that M.G. Rothschild was making the alluring offer to hand out a fine cash register to anybody who would pay $4 for a year's subscription to "America's great weekly trade journal," Mr. Mayer sat up and recalled the time about thirty years back, in Cincinnati, when one "Abe" Rothschild had shot himself in the right eye while trying to prevent his being taken back alive to Jefferson, Tex., where he had killed "Diamond Bessie" Moore in 1877.

The association of the name with the man with the counterfeit eye set Mr. Mayer busy, with the result that Inspectors Reddy and Kincaid and Detectives Nelson and McConville, after a two days' watch, got Rothschild yesterday.

This morning he will be arraigned before Commissioner Shields, with his alleged partner, Arnold G. Cahn, on the charge of using the mails with intent to defraud.

Inspector Mayer had not noticed the glass eye when the promoter of "The Successful Business Man" called on him at the end of February in regard to renting a box in the General Post office. When word reached him a few days later that a tremendous amount of mail was coming in from all points of the compass for "The Successful Business Man," he thought it was merely in reply to some advertising scheme to boom the new publication. As no complaint had been formally entered against the promoters of the new enterprise, Rothschild and his partner would probably have gathered in much more than the $7,000 they have obtained during their fortnight's pushing of the new publication, except for the mention of that eye.

Efforts to find Rothschild proved futile until yesterday noon, when he was nabbed in Broadway. At the office, at No. 302 Broadway, the inspectors and detectives also found Cahn and a woman who said she was Mrs. Rothschild. The confiscated contents of the desk revealed the promoters of "The Successful Business Man" as shrewd workers in hard times.

The bait that brought in $7,000 was the offer of a cash register, recording sales from 1 cent to $1,000, to everybody who would pay $4 for the new weekly publication designed to show merchants "how the smartest business men act." The offer made in circular letters bearing the date of February 29 was good only until March 12, when the first issue was to make its appearance. It never appeared, and the offer was extended as good until March 21, and the money continued to pour in.

When Inspector Mayer looked over Rothschild yesterday he recognized him as the "Abe" Rothschild to whom as long ago as 1896 the Fourth Assistant Postmaster General, in his annual report, gave the credit of having one of the greatest criminal careers of anybody in the United States.

To the inspector Rothschild finally admitted his identity with the son of a wealthy Cincinnati banker and jeweler who had killed "Diamond Bessie" Moore. On reaching Texas at that time he narrowly escaped lynching, but was tried and sentenced to be hanged. His family came to his defense, and after four and a half years he was acquitted. He admitted that his freedom had cost $35,000, and that he could cause a sensation by telling how he got his liberty.

Then he came to New York and was arrested for fraud in connection with the failure with liabilities of $750,000 of a business enterprise in which he was interested. He escaped conviction, took up gambling as a vocation, and was a well known figure for years at the racetracks of New York, London and Paris.

In 1889, according to his own admission, he became a professional swindler, developing a penchant for securing diamonds and other easily portable and valuable articles through the use of the mails and express railroad companies.

Arrested at San Lorenzo, Cal., on September 30, 1894, for crooked work accomplished at Moberly, Mo., in July of the same year, he escaped from a deputy marshal at Little Rock, Ark., on November 12. In March of the following year he turned up at Swainsboro, Ga., but got away with $4,400 worth of diamonds, fraudulently obtained, and was in St. Mary's, Ontario, before he was nabbed.

Brought back to Missouri, he was sentenced on March 23, 1896, to serve four years. To the postal authorities he boasted at the time of his conviction that there were at least 200 criminal charges against him in the United States, every state and territory being represented, and that he had also committed crimes up to that time in Canada, Mexico, Cuba, England and France. His whereabouts from the time of his release from the Missouri penitentiary to his arrest yesterday are unknown to Inspector Mayer.

At least 300,000 circulars a day are said to have been sent out by Rothschild since he took desk room at No. 302 Broadway. No register of the kind which this "successful business man" offered in his circulars, the inspectors say could be made for anything near the price of $4.[197]

The last reported incident involving Abe Rothschild was on July 28, 1914. According to the *New York Tribune*, he had inherited one million dollars when his mother died, and he had taken to calling himself "Major" Abe Rothschild. It was clearly a self-imposed title, since he had never served in the military, and had in fact spent a good deal of his life either in trouble or in prison. He must have felt himself invincible with the money, because he reportedly walked into a New York courtroom and

---

[197] "Abe Rothschild Again Betrayed by Glass Eye: Diamond Bessie's Slayer Caught at Get-Rich-Quick Game Here," New York *Tribune*, New York, New York, March 14, 1908.

demanded payment of a $1,300 debt supposedly owed him by the judge. Rothschild created such a scene that the judge refused to recognize him and immediately dismissed the court. At that time, Abe was under a new indictment for loan shark operations – it seems that old habits die hard, even in the face of new-found riches.[198]

But there is a question as to whether those riches actually existed or not. On January 7, 1915, the Cincinnati *Enquirer* published the following story:

Mrs. Rothschild's Will Filed

The will of Mrs. Rosa Rothschild, widow of Maier Rothschild, and who died at Atlantic City some months ago, was filed for probate her yesterday. Mrs. Rothschild left this city after the death of her husband, and been making her home in New York. The original will, which was dated June 2, 1903, gave all her personal property to her son, Charles M. Rothschild. It also provided that, from the sale of her real estate, Charles M. is to receive $65,000, and the residue of the real estate is to be divided equally between Charles M. Rothschild and her daughter, Edith Cohen, wife of Nathan D. Cohen. The will provided that if her son did not survive her, then his share was to go to his wife, Tecia Rothschild, while if her daughter did not survive her then her share was to go to her husband. The will named her son Charles and her son-in-law, Nathan D. Cohen, as executors.

On February 13, 1909, Mrs. Rothschild added a codicil to the will in which she stated that $16,000 she received from her husband's life insurance was placed by her in the hands of her son Charles, and any amount he had not used for the benefit of the estate is to go to her daughter, Mrs. Cohen, who is also to

---

[198] "Major Abe Rothschild, Once Sentenced to Hang, Risks Contempt," New York *Tribune*, New York, New York, July 28, 1914.

have a note for $4,000, executed by her brother, and all the cash on deposit in the Greenwich Savings Bank. A $1,000 United States bond is to be divided equally among her three grandchildren, Aimee Cohen and Harold and Jack Rothschild, while she disposed of her jewelry to her son, daughter and grandchildren.

The will states that no bequest is made to her son, Abe Rothschild, "for the reason that he has been the cause of so much trouble to my beloved husband and myself that I have concluded to exclude him from participation in any part of my estate."

Abe Rothschild, it will be remembered, was in considerable trouble. He was once indicted on a murder charge down in Texas, and many Cincinnatians remember of his escapades and of the "Diamond Bessie" case.

The value of Mrs. Rothschild's estate is not estimated, but, while she had no personal property here, she still owned some valuable property at Fifth and Central avenue. [199]

Perhaps Abe's earlier flaunting of his new-found wealth was premature, and the reading of the will proved to be a disappointing truth to him.

Whatever the case, there are no more newspaper records of Abe Rothschild after that day; perhaps he faded into obscurity with his fortune, or maybe the public simply grew weary of hearing of the exploits of such a scoundrel. A census Roll for New York City in 1920 shows Abe living there with a wife and two children, a son named Maier and a daughter named Rosa – which were the names of his parents. [200]

---

[199] "Mrs. Rothschild's Will Filed," The Cincinnati *Enquirer*, Cincinnati Ohio, January 7, 1915, p. 10.

[200] McKenzie, Fred. *The Abe Rothschild Story*. (Marshall, Texas: The Print Shop), 2003.

When and how Abe Rothschild died may never be known. There is, however, one legend that has been handed down through the generations in the city of Jefferson, Texas. It is said that one day a handsome, elderly man wearing a patch over his right eye came to Oakwood Cemetery and asked the caretaker there to show him the grave of Bessie Moore. Upon seeing it, he laid roses on it, knelt in prayer, commented on the goodness of the citizens to provide a decent burial, and gave the caretaker money for the future care of the grave.[201]

---

[201] Russell, Traylor. *The Diamond Bessie Murder and the Rothschild Trials.* (Waco, Texas: Texian Press). 1971.

The Curse of Diamond Bessie's Trunk

Over the years, the tragic tale of Diamond Bessie has launched many tall tales. This isn't a new phenomenon – it started with the murder itself.

Case in point... on August 17, 1880, just three years after the murder, the Leavenworth *Times* in Leavenworth, Kansas reprinted a story from the New Orleans *Times*:

Diamond Bessie's Trunk
A Relic of a Celebrated Tragedy –
Something to Steer Clear Of
At a store on Baronne Street, just adjoining Grunewald Hall, is a lady's sole leather Saratoga trunk, of the largest size, which, although entirely inoffensive in itself, and perhaps as negative a combination of sole leather, steel springs and linen as the average receptacle for feminine apparel, is nevertheless, by association, not without its history.

117

The trunk was made upon the order of a very handsome young lady, who called at the store and gave specific directions as to its interior arrangements. She appeared to be in affluent circumstances, and did not object to the price charged, which was $100. The money was paid and the trunk sent home, its owner proving to be Miss Bessie Moore, a young woman of pronounced beauty, whose career and method of earning a livelihood are not usually adopted by those of the gentler sex who consider themselves in the best society.

It appears that Miss Bessie Moore found that the trunk was not entirely to her satisfaction, and sold it back to the store at a liberal discount. She subsequently left the city for Jefferson, Texas, in company with a miscreant named Abe Rothschild, from Cincinnati. He used up her money, and with placid deviltry put a pistol to her forehead and blew out her brains. The body lay for two weeks undiscovered, and was identified by a gentleman of this city, who happened to be in Jefferson at the time.

Singularly enough, this gentleman subsequently committed suicide. Abe Rothschild was arrested in Cincinnati when in the act of attempting to commit suicide, and was sent back to Jefferson, Texas, for trial, where he now lies in jail, every influence being used to delay the trial.

The trunk was sold to a gentleman who had it thoroughly repaired. Before this gentleman had paid for the trunk he also committed suicide. It is now for sale, and, of course, is considered a prize, inasmuch as no one who has had anything to do with it, except the maker, has not died by violence.[202]

The article has a number of flaws, not the least of which is that Diamond Bessie's body was discovered by Sarah King, not

---

[202] "Diamond Bessie's Trunk," The Leavenworth *Times*, Leavenworth, Kansas, August 17, 1880, p. 1.

a man from New Orleans who happened to be in Jefferson. The fictitious man could therefore not have committed suicide.

The article states that the supposed buyer of the trunk "had it thoroughly repaired." Since (for the purpose of the article) Bessie took possession of the trunk, didn't like it, and sold it back to the shop, it would not be in need of "thorough repair."

The cursed trunk was just one tale that in today's world might be called an "urban legend."

Several rumors concerning the jury were heard. It was said, for instance, that twelve $1,000 bills were lowered into the jury room during deliberations to buy the "not guilty" verdict. Another tale is that all twelve jurors met violent deaths within a year of the trial. Still another espouses that a piano was delivered to all jurors after the trial. None of these are true, but make for colorful tales.[203]

The stories that a hack was waiting outside the door of the courthouse to take Abe swiftly away, and that the verdict was not announced until after the train whistle blew (meaning that it was just about to leave the station, allowing Abe to jump on as it pulled away) have not been substantiated. The popular rumor that Bessie was pregnant when she died has also never been proved.

The trial was so sensational, and was followed in newspapers across the nation, so it's no surprise that tall tales began to emerge.

---

[203] Russell, Traylor. *The Diamond Bessie Murder and the Rothschild Trials.* (Waco, Texas: Texian Press). 1971.

The hustling, bustling, riverport city of Jefferson in the mid-1800s

Diamond Bessie Sites Today

As the years have rolled by after the murder, many of the sites associated with the story of Diamond Bessie Moore and Abe Rothschild have disappeared into history. Others have simply changed over time, but are still locatable... at least their sites, if you know where to look. This chapter will examine the places that Bessie and Abe visited while in Jefferson, and others that are connected to the trial.

Most, if not all places, such as the Brooks House, are no longer standing. Perhaps the most elusive site is the location where Bessie was actually murdered... but we'll look at that more as we get into this intriguing chapter.

The Capitol Hotel in Marshall

Capitol Hotel, Marshall, Texas.

The Capitol Hotel from a vintage postcard

When Abe and Bessie came to Texas, their first stop was in the City of Marshall, at the Capitol Hotel where they registered as "A. Rothschild and Wife."

The Capitol Hotel was located at the corner of Bolivar and Houston Streets from the time that it was built in 1857, until it was torn down in 1971.

It was financed by George Adkins and built by slave labor, specifically Dick Land and Green Hill who were expert masons. These men made the bricks that went into the 12-inch walls of the structure.

The hotel had a fascinating history during its time. Not only did it play host to Abe Rothschild and Diamond Bessie, it was the scene of important Confederate meetings during the Civil War. For a time during the war, Marshall served as the Capital of Missouri's Confederate government-in-exile, so dignitaries from other Southern states came to the city for planning sessions, some of which were held at the hotel.

Today only the empty corner of a downtown block remains where the Capitol Hotel once stood. On the north side is a marker erected by the Texas Historical Commission to remember the old hotel.

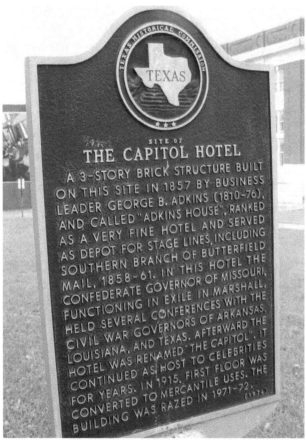

The Texas Historical Commission marker for the Capitol Hotel
on Houston St. just east of Bolivar St. in Marshall

The Jefferson T&P Train Station

Re-creation of a typical T&P Station at the Jefferson Historical Museum

When Bessie Moore and Abe Rothschild arrived in Jefferson, they took the "accommodation train" from Marshall, which carried passengers between the two cities on the Texas & Pacific Railroad tracks. The train station was located on the north side of Jefferson not far from Oakwood Cemetery on Alley Street.

You may remember from the history presented earlier that H.J. Donovan, the baggage-master of the Texas & Pacific Railroad at Jefferson, had unloaded a trunk for the couple marked "A. Moore, N.O." when they arrived in town, and then checked the same trunk through to Little Rock, Arkansas for the man when he departed.

The train station where the couple arrived is long gone, although the train tracks are still in use in Jefferson.

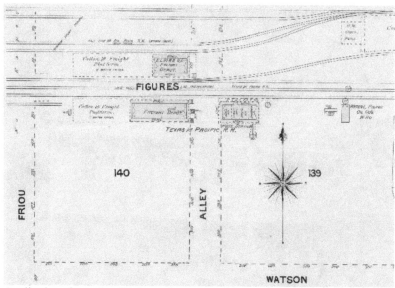

A clipping from the Sanborn Insurance Maps of the time, showing the location of the T&P train depot.

The site of the old T&P train depot today

The Brooks House

An old photo of the Brooks House on Vale Street in Jefferson

When Abe and Bessie arrived in Jefferson, they checked into the Brooks House on Vale Street, room number 4, beginning their ill-fated visit to the city.

Years later the boarding house became a private residence, which passed to a few different owners.

Tragedy struck on Sunday, August 31, 1969, when the Brooks House burned and Jefferson lost a piece of its history forever. As the story goes, the fire alarm sounded, and someone ran into the Immaculate Conception Catholic Church yelling, "The Brooks House is on fire!" It was just across the street, so the church emptied to witness the fire.

Jefferson's firemen fought the blaze gallantly, but the house was engulfed in flames and could not be saved. On that day, a piece of the city's history was lost forever.

The Brooks House burning, across the street from the Catholic Church in Jefferson (courtesy the Excelsior House Hotel)

The roof of the Brooks House engulfed in flames (courtesy the Excelsior House Hotel)

The Brooks House on fire (courtesy the Excelsior House Hotel)

128

The site of the Brooks House on Vale Street today,
with a new structure erected by the current property owner.

The Marker from the Texas Historical Commission
for the site of the Brooks House.

129

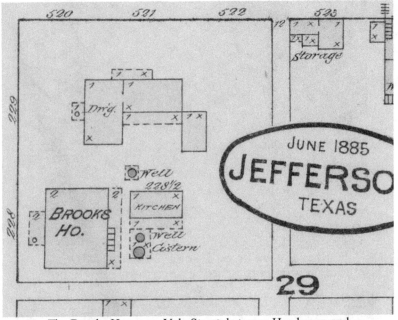

The Brooks House on Vale Street, between Henderson and
Lafayette Streets, on the 1885 Sanborn Maps of Jefferson, Texas

Mrs. Kate Wood's Restaurant

The Excelsior House Hotel, purchased in 1877 by Kate Wood

Kate Wood herself testified at Rothschild's Habeas Corpus Hearing in Jefferson, and the record is as follows: "Kate Wood kept a restaurant in Jefferson in January and February, 1877, and saw the dead woman who was found. She thought she had seen, in her restaurant, a lady very much like the deceased; but her recollection of dates and persons was indefinite, and her testimony casts no new light on the case."[204]

According to the transcript of the Court of Appeals of Texas, Dr. J.H. Turner, landlord of the Brooks House, testified that on Sunday, January 21, 1877, "Rothschild took his breakfast Sunday morning, the 21st, at the Brooks House, and that he and the lady left the house together about ten or eleven

[204] Ex Parte Abe Rothschild, Court of Appeals of Texas, 2 Tex. Ct. App. 560; 1877 Tex. Crim. App. Lexis 188, p. 4.

o'clock that morning; and about two or three o'clock in the afternoon witness next saw Rothschild in the parlor of the Hotel [the Brooks House], but the lady was not with him, and the witness saw no more of her. When Rothschild came into the parlor, witness asked him if he had had dinner, and he said he had, at Kate Wood's."

The couple had also been there earlier in the day, as reported by the Jefferson *Journal*, quoted by the Cincinnati *Enquirer*: "That morning they took a walk. Stopping at Mrs. Kate Wood's restaurant on Austin Street, they drank one or two bottles of beer. The woman exhibited suspicions of her companion, and refused to permit him to pour out the beer or to handle her glass. Her conduct toward him was strange. He tried to procure a lunch from Mrs. Wood's, but failing to get what he desired, he went over to Henriques' restaurant on Polk street, and returned with a cooked chicken, sandwiches, pickles, etc, and two bottles of beer."[205]

There can be no doubt that Kate Wood operated a restaurant at the time Abe and Bessie were in Jefferson – but the question is, where?

A Jefferson newspaper, in a December 11, 1869 issue, indicates that Kate Wood operated a restaurant at #49 Dallas Street in Jefferson. Around 1877, however, Kate Wood had acquired the Excelsior House Hotel, according to Mrs. Arch McKay and Mrs. H.A. Spellings in their book about Jefferson.[206] Fred Tarpley, Jefferson historian, also noted that "Before its acquisition by the garden club, the hotel had been owned for the longest period by Mrs. Kate Wood, a native of

[205] "Abe Rothschild: His Arrival in Jefferson, Texas," Cincinnati *Enquirer*, April 17, 1877, p. 2.
[206] McKay, Mrs. Arch, and Spellings, Mrs. H.A., *A History of Jefferson, Marion County, Texas*. (Jefferson: Christ Episcopal Church), p. 23.

Germany who bought the property in 1877 and managed it until her death in 1907."[207]

Ad for Kate Wood's Restaurant from December 11, 1869

We don't know the exact date when Mrs. Wood purchased the Excelsior House Hotel "around 1877," so it could be that the Dallas Street restaurant was where Abe and Bessie dined during their time in Jefferson, and then Mrs. Wood purchased the Excelsior House later in the year. On the other hand, she could have acquired it at the first of the year or earlier,

---

[207] Tarpley, Fred, *Jefferson: East Texas Metropolis*, (Nacogdoches: East Texas Historical Association). 1997. p. 44.

meaning that it could have just as easily been the dining room at the Excelsior House that was visited by Bessie and Abe, which was just two blocks from the Brooks House where the couple stayed.

Some sources associate the "Mrs. Kate's" from testimony to be the Excelsior House. For example, the *Paris News* of Paris, Texas reported on April 2, 1941, "One of Jefferson's most historic shrines is the old Excelsior Hotel... It was at this hostelry that Abe Rothschild told inquirers where Diamond Bessie was when she failed to return from the eventful trip across the bayou. In 1877 it was the Excelsior House, as it was the fashion to call hotels in that more hospitable, leisurely day, and was operated by Mrs. Kate Wood."[208]

The Mexia *Daily News* reported, "In 1877 the hotel was acquired by Mrs. Kate Wood. Upon her acquisition the hotel again became known as the Excelsior, and the brick portion was added...Jefferson was in its heyday in the 1870s, with a population of over 35,000. Social life was gay. The Excelsior with its beautifully appointed drawing and dining rooms, was the scene of many of the famed "Queen Mab" balls, as a part of Jefferson's own Mardi Gras."[209] It is clear from this account that she was operating a restaurant at the hotel.

Looking once again at the afore-quoted April 17, 1877 article from the Jefferson *Journal*, it said that the couple dined at "Mrs. Kate Wood's restaurant on Austin Street." This was written just three months after the alleged murder date, by a newspaper actually located in Jefferson. Even though speculation still exists, this fact lends credibility to the idea that the couple dined at the Excelsior House, and not Mrs. Wood's previous location on Dallas Street.

---

[208] Neville, A.W., "Backward Glances: Notables Who Visited Jefferson," The Paris *News*, Paris, Texas, April 2, 1941, p. 4.

[209] "Jefferson Historical Pilgrimage to be Held May 2, 3 and 4," The Mexia *Daily News*, Mexia, Texas, April 25, 1969, p. 3.

The Dining Room at Excelsior House Hotel

There is one other bit of information to consider, however. On May 1, 1875, an advertisement ran in a Jefferson newspaper for Kate Wood's "Excelsior Restaurant." While there is no address given, it is listed at "Orton's Building, Austin and Dallas Streets." Since Austin and Dallas are parallel and adjacent, this can be interpreted as a building that spans both sides of the block, with entrances on either street.

What is now the Excelsior House Hotel was named the Commercial Hotel at that time, and the Excelsior name would not come until Kate purchased the hotel in 1877.[210] It appears that she was using the name "Excelsior" for her restaurant in 1873, however, which could explain why newspapers reported that the couple dined at "Excelsior" without differentiating

---

[210] Tarpley, Fred. *Jefferson: Riverport to the Southwest.* Wolfe City, TX: Henington Pulishing Co. 1983, p. 291.

between the Excelsior House as it exists today, and Kate Wood's Excelsior Restaurant as it was prior to her purchasing the hotel.

EXCELSIOR RESTAURANT —

(Orton's building, Dallas and Austin streets,)

MRS. KATE WOOD,..............Proprietress.

FRESH OYSTERS DURING THE
SEASON.

FURNISHED ROOMS.

Day and week boarders solicited. Meals at all hours, and fare as good as the best.
May 1st. 1875.

Ad for Kate Wood's Excelsior Restaurant from May 1, 1875

There are still questions, however, that may never be answered, and speculation about the location of the restaurant of Mrs. Kate Wood where the fated couple dined while in Jefferson continues.

Kate Wood (courtesy Excelsior House Hotel)

The Rosebud Saloon

GO TO THE
ROSE BUD
＿FOR YOUR＿
Christmas Whiskey.

You will find the Best Brands
in the Market

From 75c. to $2.50 Per Quart.

any price to suit your pocket book.

DON'T FORGET
OLD PRETORIA RYE

for it will never make you cry.

Austin St., near Post Office,
Jefferson, Texas.   # CORTI & CO.

Actual newspaper ad for the Rosebud Saloon from 1904

The Rosebud Saloon is mentioned in Traylor Russell's book *The Diamond Bessie Murder and the Rothschild Trials* as one of the most popular saloons in Jefferson, and therefore most likely visited by Abe and Bessie.[211]

It also factors into the *Diamond Bessie Murder Trial* Play, as one of the characters is a bartender at the Rosebud, although the character of the bartender Morelli never testified in the actual trial.

Unfortunately the Rosebud no longer exists in Jefferson, but there are many theories about where its location might have

---

[211] Russell, Traylor. *The Diamond Bessie Murder and the Rothschid Trials* (Waco: Texian Press, 1971), p. 20.

been, placing it on this particular street or that one. Few people agree on the actual location of the Rosebud.

The first clue as to the location of the Rosebud comes from Gustav Frank's book *A Partial List of Earlier Citizens of Jefferson, Texas Compiled from Memory*. On page 67, the entry for the Rosebud Saloon reads, "Located next door to the Excelsior Hotel."[212]

Next, the Texas Historical Commission issued a historical marker for the Rosebud in 1965. The marker has long since disappeared, or was never issued, but the text proposed for the marker is on record with the Commission:

Old Rosebud Saloon
Address: Vale St. at Austin
City: Jefferson
County: Marion
Year Marker Erected: 1965
Marker Text: 1854. Rendezvous of judges, lawyers and men with notched guns. Partly burned 1902. Restored 1946. V 1965

The newspaper advertisement reproduced on the last page contains the direction, "Austin St., near Post Office, Jefferson, Texas."

A final piece of the puzzle comes from the 1890 Sanborn Maps of Jefferson. The Sanborn Map Company is an American publisher of historical and current maps of U.S. cities and towns. The maps were initially created to estimate fire insurance risks, and are known for their accuracy and therefore are a great asset to historians.

---

[212] Frank, Gustav II. *A Partial List of Earlier Citizens of Jefferson, Texas, Compiled from Memory*, (Jefferson: Marion County Genealogical Society, 1960), p. 67.

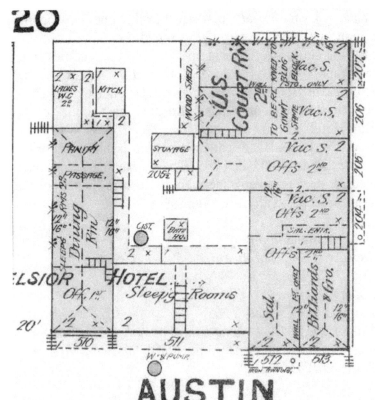

Corner of Austin and Vale Streets on the 1890 Jefferson Sanborn Maps

As shown on the above map, the Excelsior Hotel and its "sleeping rooms" occupy the western part of the block, and next door is a saloon that is annotated "sal." Given the documentation already presented, that saloon must be the Rosebud.

Whether or not Abe and Bessie were patrons there as speculated in Russell's book, and also fictitiously portrayed in the Diamond Bessie Murder Trial Play, will probably never be known. It was just a block from the Brooks House, however, and between there and what may have been "Mrs. Kate's Restaurant," the Excelsior House… so who knows?

The old Rosebud Saloon – now the annexed room of the Bayou Bakery

The interior of the Rosbud, now the Bayou Bakery, where Abe & Bessie
might have visited for a drink or two while in Jefferson

Henriques' Restaurant

After leaving Mrs. Kate's Restaurant with two bottles of beer, Abe and Bessie reportedly went to Henriques' Restaurant in Jefferson where they purchased a picnic lunch.

In her book *Some Early Citizens of Marion County, Texas*, Juanita Davis Cawthorn notes on page 38 that Isaac L. Henriques operated a grocery and retail establishment at #28 Dallas St. This is supported by an ad in the Jefferson *Jimplecute* from October 11, 1867:

Dallas Street was once a very busy street, with merchants, cotton offices and warehouses lining both sides of the street. More than once fire swept down the street, however, including a large one in 1868, and by the time that the 1885 Sanborn Insurance Maps of Jefferson were published, much of Dallas St. was vacant. It could be that Henriques merchant business was destroyed by fire, and by the time that Abe & Bessie came to town, I.L. Henrique had opened a restaurant elsewhere in town.

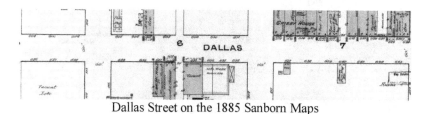

Dallas Street on the 1885 Sanborn Maps

All the white spaces on the map above are vacant lots; on the lower right side the block is simply labeled "ruins." Of the buildings still standing, the darker squares, most are labeled "vacant;" "just walls, roofless;" "vacant 1st floor;" "vacant store;" "roofless" and so forth. Dallas Street had become a ghost of the busy downtown thoroughfare that it was just a decade before.

Street numberings in downtown Jefferson have changed over the years, so it is difficult to pinpoint the exact location of where I.L. Henriques' store might have been on Dallas Street.

Perhaps the only clue is the one building from that era that is still standing – McGarity's Saloon, a.k.a. 61 Dallas St.

Since Henriques' was reportedly located at 28 Dallas, it could have been in the block across the street and down the block from McGarity's. Today there are no structures there, however.

Dallas Street today, with McGarity's Saloon (61 Dallas St.) on the right

Another problem exists, however. In the discussion of the location of "Mrs. Kate Wood's Restaurant" earlier in this chapter, the Jefferson *Journal* reported that Abe "tried to procure a lunch from Mrs. Wood's, but failing to get what he desired, he went over to Henriques' restaurant on Polk street, and returned with a cooked chicken, sandwiches, pickles, etc, and two bottles of beer." As previously stated, this was written just *three months* after the alleged murder date, by a newspaper actually located in Jefferson.

So was Henriques' Restaurant actually a retail shop located on Dallas Street, as reported in Ms. Cawthorn's book, or on Polk Street, as the Jefferson *Journal* wrote? This is a mystery that may never be solved, since there is evidence for both.

Isaac L. Henriques

Ballauf & Company Hardware

The Shreveport *Times* reported that during his initial stay in Jefferson with Diamond Bessie, Abe Rothschild was spotted going into the Ballauf & Company Hardware Store alone. The news story indicates that he purchased a pistol and cartridges there, which could have been used in the subsequent murder of Diamond Bessie. What was once Ballauf & Company Hardware is now the popular Jefferson General Store, which is located at 113 E. Austin St. in Jefferson.

Left: Balluaf Hardware in the 1800s, Right: Jefferson General Store today

☞ Send for PRICE LIST before ordering from St. Louis or New Orleans

R. BALLAUF & CO.,

DEALERS IN EVERY DESCRIPTION OF

Contractors, Blacksmiths,

MACHINISTS

TINNERS, CARPENT'RS

And Butchers Tools, Iron, Steel, Nails, Tin Plate, Copper, Lead, Zinc, and Babitt Metal; KELLY'S FAMOUS PLOWS, Stoves and Hollowware.

Sole Agents for the celebrated Avery Cast & Steel Plows, Hall's urglar Proof Safe and Lock Company and English Bellows, these goods we offer at factory prices.

FILES.—A full line always in stock, warranted equal to the best

Rubber belting, and gum packing; hemp packing, gas pipes gas pipe tongues, gas pipe stock and dies, etc.; steam pumps, steam augers, gauge cocks, and every article belonging to a mill outfit

Wagons and buggy wood material, patent wheels, iron axles, from buggy to carry log size.

Tire drills, tire-benders, tire-upsetting, tire punches; hay cutte and corn shellers of all kinds.

Superior Stoves.—Heating stoves, tinner's trimmings, tinware machinery nuts, washers & bolts, all sizes, carriage and fire bolts horse and mule shoes.

House furnishing goods, wooden pumps, pitcher pumps, thimble skeins. pipe boxes, horse shoe nails, axes, boat spikes, and a

Full Line of Hardware.

Copper, tin and sheet iron work done with neatness and dispatch nat 15 dw .

Advertisement for Ballauf & Co Hardware in
the Jefferson *Jimplecute*, November 23, 1875.

No visit to Jefferson is complete without a visit to the General Store. It has Blue Bell® Ice Cream, a full soda fountain, Jefferson's famous Moody Dogs (delicious chili dogs with a history of their own), a full array of souvenirs from tee shirts to books to handmade soap… and everything in between.

The Murder Scene

While the actual murder site may have disappeared with time, several years ago Jefferson historian Fred McKenzie set out on a quest to find it. His excursion was documented in *The Jeffersonian*, Vol. XXIII, No. 2, and *The Jeffersonian* was kind enough to allow the story to be told again here:

Much attention has been given in recent years to a murder that took place in Jefferson on January 21, 1877. Bessie Moore and Abe Rothschild came to Jefferson when it was a bustling steamboat port, and within days of their arrival, Bessie's good looks, fashionable dress and lavish diamond jewelry had earned her the nickname, "Diamond Bessie."

They were last seen together crossing the bridge over Big Cypress Bayou on their way to a picnic. No one thought too much of it at the time when Rothschild returned alone that afternoon, telling anyone who chanced to inquire that he had left his wife across the river visiting friends. Suspicions were not eve aroused when he suddenly left town two days later taking all her things with him.

However, 15 days later when Bessie's body was found on a wooded hillside near Big Cypress Bayou with a bullet in her brain, Jeffersonians were shocked and outraged.

Pretty, young Bessie Moore had been brutally murdered, execution-style, by someone, and the obvious suspect was the absent Abe Rothschild. The startling discovery of her corpse, missing for 15 days but well-preserved, was made by a black woman named Sarah King who stumbled upon it while on a hillside gathering firewood. It was said at the trial that she took a good look at the body and then "departed in a fast walk," probably one of the fastest walks ever in Marion County.

During the murder investigations and trials that followed, the murder site became well-marked, and all distances to it

149

carefully measured, recorded, and identified with existing landmarks of the era. However, as the years passed and interest waned, the knowledge of its location slipped into history.

Over time, many other changes had taken place. Old roads were abandoned and then replaced by newer highways; major power lines were built and rebuilt; excavations were made and timer was cut periodically.

As a result, there were those who said the murder site would never again be located. They were convinced that any identifiable markings had long since had been obliterated by the alterations to the terrain.

I can understand how they felt, when the new, widened business 59, abandoned roadbeds, ruins of firmer bridges and miscellaneous past and present construction sites are considered. Fortunately, all these topographical changes did not disturb the site. I found that I could take the original measurements, available from court records, and follow them to the actual spot.

An account of the journey, taken from "Centennial History of Jefferson," reads as follows: "The couple strolled leisurely along for half a mile on the other side of the bridge, then taking a path plunged into the forest, climbed a hill, almost within a stone's throw of the public thoroughfare (old Marshall Road) and within rifle shot of the city itself... their lunch was spread on a large, flat rock... deep in the heart of the woodland surrounded by the songs of birds and the musical ripple of running water, in the shade of the giant oak and ironwood (trees)...

Following these directions, I began at the foot of the present Big Cypress bridge (which is within a few feet of the original structure), and I walked a half-mile on a well-defined portion of the old Marshall Road which is still visible. I then turned right into the forest at a natural sort where a trail could have existed, then as now. I climbed a small forest-covered hill, where on the sunny side, a small, wet-weather brook courses through to the old bypass channel below. On the bank of this little brook, I located the large, flat, moss-covered rock – about 30 inches square – on which Bessie Moore and Abe Rothschild spread their picnic lunch.

Adjacent to the rock is a sizeable red oak that could have sprouted from the stump of the original "giant oak." There are several Ironwood trees in the immediate vicinity, as well as a hard maple or two, just as indicated in the early accounts of the event.

The site is located on the south side of a 55-acre tract of land known as Maison Bayou, now owned by Jan and Pete Hochendel. This parcel of land was known for years as the "old G.S. Neidermeir" tract and has been undisturbed for many years, except for occasional timber harvesting.[213]

While researching this book, I took Fred McKenzie's account of finding the gravesite, enlisted the help of Jefferson historian John Nance, secured the permission of the landowners, and spent an entire afternoon looking for the murder site. Much of the surrounding land had been cleared at that time, and at one point we found a pile of huge rocks that had been dug out of the ground. The Diamond Bessie murder site may have fallen prey to progress. In any event, we never found it, and I fear that it may be unfortunately lost to history.

In conjunction with the newspaper article previously quoted, The *Jeffersonian* printed what may be the only actual photograph of the murder site, taken during Fred McKenzie's excursion. The Historic Jefferson Foundation was kind enough to give their permission for it to be reprinted for posterity in this book.

---

[213] McKenzie, Fred. "Historian Locates Bessie Picnic Site," *The Jeffersonian*, Fall/Winter 2003, The Historic Jefferson Foundation, p. 21.

From the *Jeffersonian*: The Rock on which "Diamond" Bessie More and Abe Rothschild spread their picnic lunch before the mysterious woman was allegedly murdered by Rothschild is believed to be this one located on property belonging to Jan and Pete Hochendel, right. At left is author Jody Manley who is writing a novel based on the 1877 murder, and second from left is Fred McKenzie who located the stone. (Used with permission of the Historic Jefferson Foundation and the *Jeffersonian*)

The Marshall Courthouse

The "Little Virginia Courthouse" (courtesy of
the Inez Hatley Hughes Research Library, Marshall)

A committee was appointed by the Harrison County
Commissioners Court on April 10, 1848, to oversee the
construction of what was to be known as the "Little Virginia
Courthouse," and it would replace the original frame-and-log
building that had been used for almost ten years. The new
"Little Virginia" was to be built in the center of the town
square, with the lines of the building following those
commonly identified with government buildings in the State of
Virginia.[214] It was the site of Abe Rothschild's trial and murder
initial conviction for the crime of murder.

---

[214] Hackney, V.H., *Historical Hallmarks of Harrison County*. (Marshall,
Texas: The Marshall National Bank). 1964.

In 1887 questions about the safety of the building arose, and the Commissioners Court adopted plans for a new and enlarged courthouse that was completed in 1889. Ten years later, while workmen were repairing the building, a fire broke out and the courthouse was completely destroyed. A new courthouse was erected on the same location on the square, where it served Harrison County until 1964. At that time a modern, five-story brick building was erected on the southwest corner of the square. The "old courthouse," as it is know today, stands on the site of the "Little Virginia" and is used as a museum and offices.

The "old courthouse" in the Marshall square where the "Little Virginia" courthouse where Rothschild was tried once stood. (photo by Renee Greenwood)

The Old Jefferson Courthouse

The Courthouse where Abe Rothschild was tried in Jefferson

The old courthouse, designed by Daniel Alley and built just two blocks from the T&P Railroad line in 1870, was the location of Jefferson's famous Diamond Bessie murder trial. The building was abandoned soon after the trial completed, because the expensive building was located a mile from the heart of the business district. The Rothschild case was not only the most famous case heard in the courthouse, but the last one as well.[215]

The new Marion County Court House was completed in 1914, designed by architect Elmer George Withers. At the northern corner of the building the Dick Taylor Camp of Confederate Veterans erected a monument to honor the county's dead in the American Civil War.

---

[215] Tarpley, Fred. *Jefferson: Riverport to the Southwest.*(Wolfe City, Texas: Henington Pulishing Co.). 1983, p. 147.

The old courthouse soon fell into disrepair. In an attempt to save it, the building was converted into an African-American public school for Jefferson. In 1937, the building burned, and was a total loss.[216]

Today the Primary Campus for the Jefferson Independent School District, along with the Marion County Appraisal District, occupies the site of the original Marion County Courthouse where Abe Rothschild was acquitted.

Site of the old courthouse in Jefferson on Highway 49

[216] Tarpley, Fred. *Jefferson: Riverport to the Southwest*.(Wolfe City, Texas: Henington Pulishing Co.). 1983, p. 148.

Diamond Bessie's Grave

On February 7, two days after its discovery, the body of Diamond Bessie was buried in Jefferson's Oakwood Cemetery. The residents of the city took up a collection of $150 for a casket and burial, and erected a small slab over the grave.[217]

Because of the national notoriety of the trial, Diamond Bessie became quite a celebrity in death. In 1878, The *Times-Picayune* newspaper in New Orleans reported:

The grave of Bessie Moore, the murdered victim of Abe Rothschild, is visited by nearly every traveler who stops at Jefferson. The people gave the murdered girl a Christian sepulchre, a nice metallic coffin being used and no expense

---

[217] Russell, Traylor. *Carpetbaggers, Scalawags & Others*. (Jefferson, Texas: Marion County Historical Survey Committee), 1973. p. 81.

spared in the funeral. At the head of the grave is a marble slab with the simple inscription "Bessie."[218]

One story that has continued to be handed down through the years comes from the 1890s, when Abe Rothschild is said to have made a final visit to Jefferson. According to F.B. Schweers, whose father was the caretaker of Oakwood Cemetery when Diamond Bessie was buried there, one day a handsome and elderly man visited the cemetery, and asked him where the grave of Diamond Bessie was. When the elder Clemens A. Schweers pointed the way, the stranger laid a wreath of roses on the grave and knelt in prayer. When he finally rose, the stranger asked who had paid the burial expense, and Schweers explained that the citizens of Jefferson had taken up a collection. The stranger nodded, and then gave Schweeres ten dollars and departed. Some say that it was Abe Rothschild, come to pay his final respects, others believe that it was Bessie's father. No one knows for sure who the mysterious stranger was.[219]

Over the years, the ravages of time took a toll on the slab, and the lettering on it became unreadable. One evening in November 1933, sometime between sundown and sunup the next day, something mysterious occurred... a new marker appeared on the grave. It had a diamond chiseled into the stone with the words: "Bessie Moore, Dec 31, 1876." Although no one knew where the marker came from or who erected it, most people believed that the inscription was meant to indicate the date of her death. The date was erroneous, but the sentiment was heart-felt by the community.[220]

---

[218] "Texas," The *Times-Picayune*, New Orleans, Louisiana, Jan 1 1878, p. 6
[219] Russell, Traylor. *The Diamond Bessie Murder and the Rothschild Trials.* (Waco, Texas: Texian Press), 1971, p. 104.
[220] "Backward Glances: Diamond Bessie Murder Case" The Paris News, Paris, Texas, April 11, 1941, p.4

Eight years later in 1941, ironworker Ed McDonald revealed himself as the benefactor, saying that he did it to get the town talking.[221] In an interview, McDonald stated, "I placed it there one night because it did not seem right for Diamond Bessie to sleep in an unmarked grave."[222]

It is said that McDonald also quietly put roses on the grave from time to time, leading to the legend that "an unseen hand periodically placed flowers on the grave of Diamond Bessie."

In the 1960s the Jessie Allen Wise Garden Club built a wrought iron fence around the grave and put a bench there for visitors to rest.[223]

A metal plaque was attached to the fence bearing the same date as the tombstone: December 31, 1876, instead of the actual date of death, which is believed to be January 21, 1877.

[221] Morthland, John. "Cemeteries: The Plots Thicken At Five Final Resting Places That Are Simply To Die For," *Texas Monthly*, March 1999.

[222] Tarpley, Fred. *Jefferson: Riverport to the Southwest*. (Wolfe City, Texas: Henington Publishing Company), 1983.

[223] Harvey, Mary-Margaret. *The History of the Jessie Allen Wise Garden Club, Continued*. (Jefferson: The Jessie Allen Wise Garden Club), 2013.

Note from the author: At this point, I have to step away from my role as the writer, and tell you a personal story. Several years ago I was working on a book called "Ghosts of East Texas and the Pineywoods," and along with all the ghost stories I included several of Jefferson's more mysterious tales, including that of Diamond Bessie. In closing the chapter, I said that "an unseen hand places flowers on the young woman's grave..." Fast forward several years, and I was out around town with my wife, and she asked if we could cruise Oakwood Cemetery. I love going there, and have spent hours reading the tombstones and photographing the statuary, so I told her that it wouldn't be a problem at all. As we entered the cemetery, I asked her what she wanted to see. She said, "I just need to check the flowers on Diamond Bessie's grave." Looking a little confused, I asked, "Why?" She shrugged and replied, I'm the chairman of the Garden Club committee that keeps flowers on her grave throughout the year." It was all that I could do to keep from slamming on the brakes; I said, "You mean that YOU'RE the unseen hand?!?" True story.

To this day there is a committee in the Garden Club that keeps flowers on Diamond Bessie's grave, including roses during Jefferson's annual Pilgrimage, when the final trial of Abe Rothschild is put on as a light-hearted production.[224]

But the Jessie Allen Wise Garden Club isn't the only one leaving objects on Bessie's grave. Throughout the year visitors to Jefferson come to Oakwood Cemetery to pay their respects to Diamond Bessie. People leave all sorts of things, from coins to stuffed animals, costume jewelry to flowers. The one thing that never happens is any vandalism or disrespect to the grave – people seem to have an undying respect for the young lady who was so brutally murdered all those years ago.

---

[224] Harvey, Mary-Margaret. *The History of the Jessie Allen Wise Garden Club, Continued.* (Jefferson: The Jessie Allen Wise Garden Club), 2013.

Beads draped on the tombstone during Jefferson's Mardi Gras celebration

The leaving of mementos on the final resting places of people dates back to the beginning of time. Excavations of even the earliest graves uncover goods meant to serve the deceased in the next world, such as pottery, weapons and beads. The earliest known coins that have been left at a grave date to the late seventh century B.C. As societies began embracing monetary systems, coins began being left in the graves of its citizens merely as yet another way of equipping the dear departed in the afterlife. In these modern days, coins and other small items are sometimes discovered on grave markers. These small tokens are left by visitors for no greater purpose than to indicate that someone has visited that particular grave. It has long been a tradition among persons of the Jewish faith, for example, to leave a small stone or pebble atop a headstone just to show that someone who cared had stopped

161

by. Coins (especially pennies) are favored by others who wish to demonstrate that the deceased has not been forgotten or in the case of Diamond Bessie, that someone just wanted to pay their respects.[225]

Coins left on the grave by visitors to the cemetery

There are some people who have started their own Diamond Bessie tradition. Every year during the holiday season, several plastic Champaign glasses are found one morning around the grave. While the actual date that it happens is a mystery, this has been going on for a number of years now, and one can only presume that a small group of people meet out at Bessie's grave to have a toast. The real question is, do they pour one of the glasses for Diamond Bessie herself?

---

[225] Mikkelson, Barbara, "Coined Tradition," *Snopes.com*, 5/18/2014, accessed 4/26/2015, www.snopes.com/military/coins.asp.

The mysterious Champaign glasses around Bessie's grave one year

Diamond Bessie's grave is easy to find. From the intersection of Highway 49 (Broadway St.) and Alley St. in Jefferson, go north on Alley. You'll cross several railroad tracks. As you do so, you're actually passing the location of the old T&P railroad station where Abe and Bessie first arrived in Jefferson; there's nothing but dirt and grass there now.

After passing the railroad tracks, you'll see one of Jefferson's water towers – the cemetery entrance is just behind it. Turn right on Webster Street and enter the main gate of Oakwood Cemetery. Follow that road into the cemetery until you dead end. Look to your right, and you'll see the grave of Diamond Bessie Moore with a black fence around it, and a concrete bench where you can rest for a moment and pay your respects to Jefferson's adopted daughter, who rests in the shade of the magnolia trees.

163

Map of Oakwood Cemetery showing Diamond Bessie's Grave:

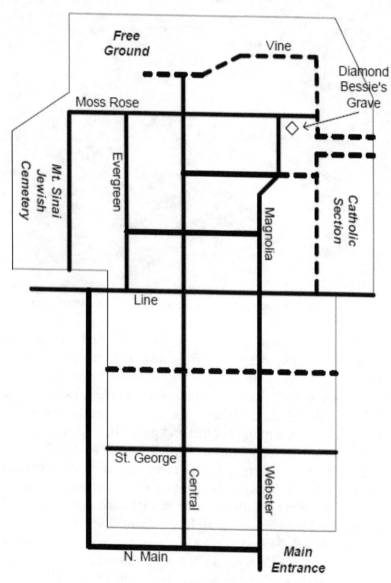

From the 2014 performance: Joe Lee as Judge B.T. Estes,
Chris Freeman as Bailiff, Bruce Abraham as the Prosecuting Attorney,
and Brooke Bradley as Isabella Gouldy.

The Diamond Bessie
Murder Trial© Play

The ultimate tribute to the memory of Diamond Bessie is the annual play that bears her name: The Diamond Bessie Murder Trial©, written by Mrs. Lawton Riley and first staged in 1955.

It has been performed every year since, during Jefferson's Historical Pilgrimage the first weekend in May, and has featured some of Jefferson's most prominent citizens as actors.

The initial research on the play was done by William J. Cornelius, a Jefferson attorney at the time, who sifted through the original court records to glean items of testimony that could be used for the play. He turned this material over to Mrs. Lawton Riley, wife of the priest at Jefferson's Christ Episcopal Church, who wrote the script for the play.

PAGE 1a

CERTIFICATE OF REGISTRATION
OF A CLAIM TO COPYRIGHT IN A DRAMATIC OR A DRAMATICO-MUSICAL COMPOSITION

REGISTRATION NO.   CLASS

Dc   39120   **D**

THIS IS TO CERTIFY that the following statements for the work herein named have been made a part of the records of the Copyright Office. In witness whereof the seal of the Copyright Office is hereto affixed.

Arthur Pile

Register of Copyrights
United States of America

1. COPYRIGHT CLAIMANT OR CLAIMANTS (Full NAMES and ADDRESSES):

   MRS. LAWTON RILEY (PEN NAME PAT O'NEELE)

   P.O.BOX 254, JEFFERSON, TEXAS

2. TITLE OF WORK DIAMOND BESSIE MURDER TRIAL

3. AUTHORS (The word "author" includes an employer in the case of works made for hire). Full name, pseudonym, if any, and year of birth are requested for cataloging purposes. If the work is a dramatico-musical composition indicate which of the authors is the composer of the music. Citizenship *must* be given.

   (a) Name LOUISE   O'CALLAGHAN   RILEY Citizenship AMERICAN
          (First)   (Middle)   (Last)   (Give name of country)

   Domicile JEFFERSON, TEXAS   Birth 1902
               (Address)   (Year)

   (b) Name   Citizenship
         (First)   (Middle)   (Last)   (Give name of country)

   Domicile   Birth
               (Address)   (Year)

   (c) Name   Citizenship
         (First)   (Middle)   (Last)   (Give name of country)

   Domicile   Birth
               (Address)   (Year)

4. FOR PUBLISHED WORKS ONLY (Date first placed on sale, sold, or publicly distributed). Fill in either (a) or (b):

   (a) If first published in the United States
                  (Month, day, and year)

   (b) If first published outside the United States:

                   at
   (Month, day, and year)   (City and country)

5. SEND CERTIFICATE TO: (If refund or other communications are to be sent to another person, give his name in space 6.)

   Name

   Address
              (Number and street)

DATES OF RECEIPT IN COPYRIGHT OFFICE

APPLICATION FEB -7 1955 FEB 2 1955

ONE COPY FEB -7 1955

TWO COPIES

FEE 9348 FEB -7 '55

TURN THIS PAGE

6. Name   Address
   (City)   (Zone)   (State)

Mrs. Lawton Riley's Copyright Registration for the Play

166

On February 29, 1956, Mrs. Lawton Riley signed an agreement with the Jessie Allen Wise Garden Club, saying, "It is understood and agreed that for $1.00 and other good and valuable consideration I do hereby relinquish or sell to the Jessie Allen Wise Garden Club all copyrights and rights of performance of the script, known as the "Diamond Bessie Murder Trial" which I wrote for the Garden Club in 1955.[226]

The prosecuting and defense attorneys were only given questions for the trial in the initial script. The rest of their part, including the summations, were left to their own ad-lib. In the first two productions, Joe McCasland played the prosecuting attorney and William Parker played the defense attorney. Mahlon Walters then took over the role of the defense attorney, and it is said that McCasland and Walters would meet each year at Mahlon's law office at the corner of Austin and Vale streets to plan what they were going to do in the play. They were supposedly very competitive – if McCasland did a forty-five minute summation, Walters would go for forty-six.

The original script also had no testimony by the Sheriff; he was instead simply used to move characters in and out of the production. This was actually an important job – the play was performed at the old Jewish Synagogue in Jefferson, which had been locked for over 35 years. Although the Jessie Allen Wise Garden Club would purchase and restore the building in 1966, during the first few performances only the auditorium was usable. A school bus was parked outside, where the cast would wait for their turn to take the stage. The sheriff would come and get each actor when it was his or her time to perform, and lead them into the "courtroom." At one performance, Mahlon Walters, instead of going into his defense summation, called Sheriff John Vines to the stand. Cordell Ogburn was playing

---

[226] Letter from Mrs. Riley to Mrs. Jack Ford, President of the Jessie Allen Wise Garden Club, dated February 29, 1956.

the sheriff, and had no idea what was going on. Defense Attorney Walters proceeded to question the sheriff for half an hour, asserting that he was actually the father of Jennie Simpson, the chambermaid of the Brooks Hotel who testified earlier in the play. Cordell, the actor, was becoming angrier and angrier, and the Defense Attorney pushed him right up to the brink. After that, the testimony of the Sheriff was a permanent fixture in the play.

The Diamond Bessie Murder Trial Cast Photo from 1963

When Dwayne Dennis took over the role of sheriff, Bill Cornelius as the Defense Attorney asked the question: "You've been Sheriff for twenty years at $20 a month, and you've become a millionaire? Now tell me, just how did you do that?" The original answer from the Sheriff Vines character was, "Well, it wasn't easy!" Over the years the answer has morphed into a response that reflects headlines from the local or national news.

For example, the year that Viagra came on the scene, the Sheriff answered, "Well, I invested all my money into a little blue pill."

When Donald Trump was sinking a lot of cash into investigating President Obama's place of birth, the Sheriff said, "I've been working for Trump, looking into some kind of birth certificate thing."

The year after Janet Jackson's "wardrobe malfunction" at the Super Bowl XXXVIII, the Sheriff answered, "I've been making extra money as Janet Jackson's wardrobe consultant."

The answer as to how the Sheriff got rich changes every year, and is never revealed – even to the other cast members – until the first night of the play.

From the 1974 performance: Bill Cornelius as the Defense Attorney, Joe Limberg as the Judge, George Dupree as the Bailiff, and Tony Hileman as the Prosecuting Attorney

From the 1962 performance: Marie Durrum as Isabella Gouldy
and Joe McCasland as the Prosecuting Attorney

There was no heat or air conditioning in the playhouse when the play first began, so the audience was subjected to the whims of the weather. George Haggard, who played the part of the coroner and also owned the local funeral home, would put up a funeral tent by the front door in case it rained.

Attendance was sparse for the first few years; the play did not attract the sell-out crowds that it would in the future.

There were originally gas lights in the playhouse, which the character of the janitor would light at the first of the play, and they would burn during the entire performance. Once air conditioning was added to the building, the gas lights had to be turned out when the play began because the air would keep extinguishing them, but the gas would keep flowing.

Gradually, humor began to creep into the play, especially when Tony Heilman took over the role of the Prosecuting Attorney. Tony took every opportunity to add a joke here and there, and Bill Cornelius, who had taken up the role of Defense Attorney, began to play along.

Slowly but surely, the audiences increased. Initially the play was done on Friday and Saturday nights. At one point a Sunday afternoon performance was added, and then a second Saturday play, and then it moved onto Thursday as well. For a period of time there was a Wednesday performance for locals, and friends and family of the actors. Unlike the other performances, this one had many inside jokes and references that would only be appreciated by the people of Jefferson. Eventually the Wednesday performance was discontinued.

From the 2014 performance: Chris Freeman as the Bailiff, and your author, Mitchel Whitington, as Sheriff John Vines

171

From the 2014 Performance: Becky Palmer as the Ghost of Diamond Bessie, and David Ham as Abe Rothschild. This is Ms. Palmer's final performance after thirty years in the roll.

Originally the synagogue/playhouse could accommodate an audience of 150 people, including the balcony. In 2004, the walls of the building were starting to sag, and an architectural evaluation was performed. The results showed that the playhouse was in desperate need of restoration, and the Jessie Allen Wise Garden Club began the project. For 2005 and 2006, the production was moved to the Marion County Courthouse while work was being done on the playhouse.

After the restoration, the audience capacity was reduced to ninety people and the balcony was reserved for lighting, the organ, and other mechanical equipment.

The jury for the play is provided by the Jefferson Lions Club. Occasionally, however, someone will be sick, or detained at work, or have some other reason that they can't make the play. There have been times when the jury wrangler has stepped inside the playhouse, surveyed the crowd, and found a volunteer to serve jury duty. On such occasions, there has been a juror who takes the stage in short pants or tennis shoes.

And of course, a play couldn't go on for over half a century without some jokes being played among the cast members.

For example, when Sam Hall was playing the Prosecuting Attorney, he was a teetotaler and didn't drink at all. Just before the play, however, another cast member snuck in and substituted a glass of vodka for his regular glass of water. When he picked it up in the course of the play and took a sip, he spit, gagged, and took a full ten minutes to regain his composure.

Whenever a pastor from one of the local churches served in the jury, either the prosecuting or defense attorney would make a joke associating them with either Morelli's Rosebud Saloon or the tainted angel of the play Isabella Gouldy. One year when the pastor of the First Baptist Church was in the jury and had taken a lot of ribbing from the attorneys over the course of the production, he introduced himself after the play by saying, "I *used* to be pastor of FBC here in Jefferson."

One of the current Abe Rothchild actors is David Ham, and he followed the long tradition of other Abes of moving the eye patch from one side to the other when returning to the "courtroom" for the final verdict. After doing it at one performance, David actually received a letter from the Jessie Allen Wise Garden Club instructing him to never, ever do that again. David continues to move the eye patch to this very day.

Every actor who has been with the play for any length of time has a story about the pranks. When Milton Jones (who supplied a lot of information for this chapter) was playing the role of the Judge, he would call for the verdict from the jury, and the foreman would hand a piece of paper to the Bailiff who would pass it over to him. Milton said that over the years, he was handed all manner of things from the jury foreman, including risqué photos of women. He received any and everything except the verdict. Finally he started printing out the verdict and giving it to the jury before they went back in, but the paper he got back was never what he had given them.

The jury isn't exempt from the odd things that happen behind the scenes in the play. For example, Jefferson ISD CFO Mike Wood was serving on the jury as the foreman one evening, when his wife Leslie showed up at the playhouse to say that she'd accidentally locked herself out of their house. A note was written that his wife needed his keys, and the actress playing Isabella Gouldy took it up and slipped it to Mike when she took the stand. He opened it, read it, laughed, and then tucked it away – he thought that it was a joke. Isabella whispered, "No, I'm not kidding, Leslie's locked out of the house!" Mike gave Isabella the keys, and after her testimony, she took them back to Leslie with the audience none the wiser.

The cast relaxing between Saturday performances, 2015.

As your humble author, who has played the role of Sheriff John Vines for a number of years, even I have a story to tell. A friend of mine, Bob Avery, took over the role of Prosecuting Attorney when the regular actor Bruce Abraham was sick one year. Bob was talking a little low, so the director, Bobbie Hardy, asked me to slip him a note asking him to speak up a bit. I did so between witnesses, and Bob started doing a great job after that. It worked so well, in fact, that I couldn't resist writing a new note that said, "Your fly is open," which I put in his hand after the next witness. I stood at the back of the playhouse and watched my friend turn around as casually as he possibly could to check the fly on his trousers, and then look back and glare at me when he realized that I was just having a little fun with him.

From the 2012 performance: The jury and Judge Bill Cornelius as the Defense Attorney. This was Judge Cornelius' 50th anniversary play performance in that role, and his final appearance in the Diamond Bessie Murder Trial play.

Skip Torrans, the 2013 Jury Wrangler, giving final instructions
before the jury is seated. Standing in the back is Jim Finstrom,
playing the part of the Defense Attorney.

Jefferson is a city of incredible history, and after over sixty consecutive years of performances, the Jessie Allen Wise Garden Club's production of the Diamond Bessie Murder Trial has certainly become a part of that legacy.

In all those performances, the names and faces of the actors have changed over the years, and many are immortalized on the back wall photographs in the playhouse. The characters in the play have never changed, however – there have been no additions or deletions. The character list that follows is the same in the latest performance as it was in the first one.

The director of the play is a pivotal person in the production, sending out letters at the first of the year, recruiting new actors when necessary, and keeping the play on track. It's only right to give credit to those who have kept the play going over the years. Diamond Bessie would be proud.

Director Bobbie Hardy with Bill Cornelius at his 50th year performance in the Diamond Bessie Murder Trial play as the Defense Attorney in 2012.

Diamond Bessie Play Directors Throughout the Years

George Blackwood (1955)
Mary Evelyn Womack (1956)
Faun Shaw (1957)
George Blackwood (1958-61)
Mrs. J. Byron Parker (1962)
Mrs. Greer Dowell (1963)
Faun Shaw (1964-1985)
William J. Cornelius (1986)
Faun Shaw (1987)
Marcia Thomas (1988)
Joyce Ball (1989-1990)
Faun Shaw (1991)
Martha Spell (1992)
Faun Shaw (1993-1995)
Margaret Jones (1996-2008)
Bobbie Hardy (2009-present)

A 2011 Diamond Bessie cast curtain call.

Cast of the play
(in order of appearance)

Sam, the Gravedigger
Abe Rothschild
Jim, a boy at the cemetery
Ghost of Diamond Bessie
Sheriff John Vines
The Janitor
The Bailiff/Court Reporter
Judge B.T. Estes
Defense Attorney David B. Culberson
Prosecuting Attorney George T. Todd
Jennie Simpson, a maid at the Brooks House
Isabella Gouldy, a "lady" about town
Antonio A. Morelli, owner of The Rosebud Saloon
Justice Bankstead, the county coroner
and of course, the Jury

From the 2012 performance: Karl Fredrickson as Sam the Gravedigger, Jeff Taylor as Abe Rothschild and Caiden Phillips as Jim.

Most of the characters in the play are historical figures that played an actual part in the trial: Abe Rothschild, John Vines, Judge Estes, Defense Attorney Culberson, Prosecuting Attorney Todd, Jennie Simpson, and Isabella Gouldy.

A few of the characters are simply generic people to move the story along: Jim, the boy at the cemetery; the janitor; the court reporter; and of course, the jury.

Diamond Bessie's murder was the impetus for the entire play, so it's only appropriate that her character is there, if only as a ghost.

Three of the characters are loosely based on real people. Sam the gravedigger is much like Clemens A. Schweers, who was the caretaker of the cemetery when the mysterious man who many believe to be Rothschild came and asked for directions to Bessie's grave.

Antonio A. Morelli, bartender/owner of The Rosebud Saloon in the play, is probably based on the real-life saloon keeper who was called to testify, John Neff. Unlike his dramatic counterpart, Neff was simply to testify that Rothschild was in his saloon drinking on the night of the alleged murder. He was a witness called by the defense instead of the prosecution as the play depicts.

And finally, Justice Bankstead is actually based on the Marion County corner at the time of the murder, C.C. Beckford.

Several members of the cast, makeup crew, and jury from the 2012 production of the play. L to R: Bob Flanders, Mickie Moore, Mitchel Whitington, Skip Torrans, Bobbie Hardy, Trevor McNeely, Bill Cornelius, Chris Freeman, Don Oatman, David Ham, Georgette Freeman, Ashley Moore, Hollis Shadden, and Bob Nickel.

After one studies the facts of the case, it is clear that even the whimsical adaptation of the Abe Rothschild trial as is portrayed in the Diamond Bessie Murder Trial© contains many elements of truth about the entire affair… which may be why it has been enjoyed by audiences for so many years.

From the 2012 performance: Joe Lee as Judge B.T. Estes,
Chris Freeman as Bailiff, Bruce Abraham as the Prosecuting Attorney,
Jack Rasberry as the Coroner, and Michael Martin as the Jury Foreman.

Diamond Bessie Characters in the 2014 Pilgrimage Parade: Joe Lee, Brooke Bradley, David Ham, Mitchel Whitington, Jim Finstrom, and David Little. The playhouse is in the background.

The full stage setting from the 2012 performance: David Ham as Abe Rothschild, Joe Lee as Judges Estes, Chris Freeman as the Bailiff, and Larry Johnson as Justice Bankstead.

The author as Sheriff John Vines, ready for the Diamond Bessie play

Afterword by the Author

I've spent a very long time with Abe and Bessie – well, at least figuratively, I guess. My interest was first piqued in the whole affair over a decade ago when I started serving in the jury for the *Diamond Bessie Murder Trial* play. When I took over the role of sheriff in 2009, I knew that at some point I was going to write a book about the real events – not just the fanciful tales that have been told over the years.

In doing that, I've read every possible work on the case that I could find, studied some of the original court transcripts, and sifted through I-don't-know-how-many newspaper articles from the day. During this time I have, of course, formed my own opinions as to what actually happened, and who did what to whom.

To begin with, it's clear that Bessie Moore (a.k.a. Annie Stone) and Abe Rothschild were both shady characters, using a string of aliases – even on their marriage license. They signed into the Brooks House in Jefferson under an alias as well – "A. Monroe and wife." This is strange since Abe used his real name only a night or so before in Marshall, Texas... unless, he was already planning to murder Bessie in Jefferson, and was starting to cover his trail at that point.

They were spotted walking across the bridge over Big Cypress Bayou carrying a picnic lunch, and Abe was seen without Bessie later that day. He then gave conflicting stories as to where she was. First he said the Bessie was at Mrs. Kate's Restaurant – possibly the Excelsior House – but then he later changed his story to say that she was staying with friends on the other side of the bayou.

Abe then boarded the first passenger train out of town, and he was seen carrying Bessie's luggage.

And then there is the trail of diamonds... first they were seen on Bessie's fingers before she disappeared, then on Abe's at the Brooks House Hotel after he returned without his wife, and then Abe pawned them in St. Louis after leaving Jefferson on the way back to Cincinnati.

Bessie's body was found wearing the clothes that she had on when walking across the bayou with Abe. If she did stay behind with friends, did she really wear the same outfit and underclothes for a week or more? With no money, where did she eat, where did she sleep? The only witness that claimed to have seen her after Abe's departure was Isabella Gouldy, who fled justice after being accused of perjury, which brings everything she said into question.

All this is curious, but the point that Abe Rothschild was basically acquitted on was the lack of decomposition of the body. Could the corpse have lain in the woods for two weeks and looked as good as it reportedly did? In January, with a snow, I can imagine that it could.

Edward Mondor, associate professor of insect ecology at Georgia Southern University, was quoted by the Weather Channel as saying, "Temperature is the number one thing that influences the rate of [body] decomposition, affecting the bacteria and insects that aid in the process."[227]

"Weather plays a huge role," says Daniel J. Wescott, director of the Forensic Anthropology Center at Texas State University. "If it's too cold the insects won't be active. If it's too hot, it'll kill off the insects."[228]

There was much debate about whether the weather had been colder or warmer than normal, and exactly when there was snowfall and how long it was on the ground, but at the end of the day we're still talking about January in East Texas. Although there were no official records kept of the temperature in Jefferson at that time, the woman who discovered the body was out gathering firewood because of the cold weather. The trial transcripts indicate that when the body was brought indoors to the Coroner's office where it was warm, it began to deteriorate quite rapidly.

And what of Abe's suicide attempt? In the role that I play of Sheriff John Vines in the *Diamond Bessie Murder Trial* play, the prosecuting attorney asks me the question, "Innocent men don't try to kill themselves, do they?" To which my scripted answer is "They sure don't!"

In reality, though, if Abe hadn't been haunted by the memories of his actions back in Jefferson, why would he try to

---

[227] Burger, Michelle, "From Flesh to Bone: The Role of Weather in Body Decomposition," *Weather.com*, 10/31/2013, accessed 06/14/2015, www.weather.com/science/news/flesh-bone-what-role-weather-plays-body-decomposition-20131031.

[228] Ibid.

take his own life? And once imprisoned, why would there be two different attempts to break him out?

For the most part, the evidence is circumstantial. There are no eyewitness, no smoking gun, and the State of Texas still lists the crime as unsolved…. yet I believe in my heart that Abe Rothschild killed his wife, Diamond Bessie Moore, on Sunday, January 21, 1877, and left her body lying in the woods south of Jefferson.

It is the only explanation that completes the story. And although Bessie Moore, or Annie Stone, was a bit of a "tainted angel," the citizens of Jefferson back in the day banded together to take care of her burial, mark her grave, and preserve her memory.

As a part of the Jefferson community today, I feel a similar obligation. Perhaps now that the book is finished, I'll go by the local florist, then drive out to Oakwood Cemetery and lay a simple rose on her grave. I think that Bessie deserves at least that.

A Timeline of Bessie and Abe

1854 – Annie Stone (a.k.a. Diamond Bessie Moore) is born in Syracuse, NY.

1875 – Bessie and Abe were seen drunk and fighting in Cincinnati, OH.

1876 – The couple was in New Orleans, and Bessie pawned her luggage for them to get back to Cincinnati.

1876 – Abe pimped Bessie out at the National Republican Convention in Cincinnati.

1876 – Bessie moved to Chicago, followed by Abe, where she worked in several houses of prostitution.

01/10/1877 – Abe and Bessie married in Danville, Illinois, just south of Chicago.

01/11/1877 – Bessie left Chicago accompanied by Abe, headed for Texas.

01/17/1877 – They arrived in Marshall, Texas, where they signed in at the Capitol Hotel as "A. Rothschild & Wife."

01/19/1877 – Abe and Bessie arrived in Jefferson, signing in at the Brooks House as "A. Monroe & wife."

01/21/1877 – The couple took breakfast at the Brooks House, walked around town, and then were seen walking over the Big Cypress Bayou bridge for a picnic. Abe returned alone.

01/22/1877 – Abe spent the day at the Brooks House - no trains departed that day.

01/23/1877 – Abe departed Jefferson with Bessie's baggage on the first train out of town since Sunday the 21st.

02/05/1877 – Bessie's body was discovered in the woods near Jefferson.

02/06/1877 – A Coroner's Inquest was held in Jefferson concerning the murder.

02/17/1877 – Abe attempted suicide on the steps of Aug's Clubhouse in Cincinnati.

03/16/1877 – Abe was arrested in Cincinnati, and a hearing was held concerning that arrest.

03/19/1877 – John Vines telegraphed the Mayor of Jefferson, saying that the matter had been settled and that Rothschild could be extradited in twenty days.

04/05/1877 – John Vines left Cincinnati for Jefferson with Abe Rothschild.

04/07/1877 – Rothschild arrived in Jefferson and is put in jail.

04/26/1877 – An indictment was returned by the Marion County Grand Jury against Abe Rothschild.

05/04/1877 – The first indictment was dismissed on the grounds that it was defective and could not return a judgment of conviction, so a second indictment was returned by the Grand Jury.

05/24/1877 – The trial began in Jefferson.

05/25/1877 – The court granted a continuance in the case to the defense, delaying the trial until the next court term.

08/15/1877 – The Habeas Corpus Hearing was held, where bail was denied.

12/17/1877 – The trial resumed in Jefferson.

01/02/1878 – Another continuance was granted in the trial.

05/07/1878 – The trial resumed in Jefferson.

05/15/1878 – A Change of Venue was granted, moving the trial to Harrison County.

12/17/1878 – The trial resumed in the new venue of Marshall, Texas.

12/24/1878 – A verdict of guilty was returned in the trial, with a mandatory death sentence.

11/20/1879 – Rothschild's case was heard before the Court of Appeals in Tyler.

01/14/1880 – The Court of Appeals in Tyler reversed the guilty verdict.

12/01/1880 – A new indictment was returned in Marion County.

12/16/1880 – The second trial began in Marion County.

12/30/1880 – A verdict of not guilty was returned by the jury.

Index

Abraham, Bruce, 165, 175, 181
Adams, Archie, 91
Adkins, George, 122
Aetna House, 21
Anderson, Evelyn, 11
Armistead, W.T., 25, 59
Atlanta Constitution, 104, 105
Atlanta, Georgia, 103
Aug's Clubhouse, 36, 188
Augusta, Georgia, 104
Austin Dispatch, 95
Austin Weekly Statesman, 57, 83, 84, 85, 202, 203, 204
Avery, Bob, 175
Bagby, Sheriff, 51
Ball, Joyce, 177
Ballauf & Company Hardware, 26, 146
Barrymore, Maurice, 74
Belmont, Josephine, 11
Bickford, Judge, 6, 32, 37, 39, 41
Big Cypress Bayou, 5, 8, 27, 32, 184, 188
Blackwood, George, 177
Booty, Judge A.J., 75, 83, 88, 89

Bradley, Brooke, 165, 182
Bradstreet Business Listing, 103
Brooks House Hotel, 15, 17, 23, 24, 25, 28, 30, 32, 36, 38, 44, 52, 65, 67, 76, 77, 91, 121, 126, 127, 128, 129, 130, 131, 132, 134, 140, 178, 184, 188
Brown, A.P., 90, 91
Cahn, Arnold G., 111
Campbell, T.J., 57, 59
Capitol Hotel, 35, 36, 76, 122, 123, 188
Cass County, Texas, 17, 73
Charleston, South Carolina, 104
Chatham, Jimmie Fay, 69
Chicago Daily Tribune, 95
Chicago Inter Ocean, 83, 86, 95, 204
Chicago, Illinois, 13, 98
Christ Episcopal Church, 132, 166, 202
Cincinnati Enquirer, 13, 20, 38, 49, 56, 65, 72, 79, 87, 92, 93, 95, 114
Cincinnati, Ohio, 10, 11, 12, 13, 14, 16, 17, 18, 20, 21, 22, 36, 37, 38, 41, 48,

Bibliography

"A Batch of Texas News Products," The *Times-Picayune*, New Orleans, Louisiana, January 1, 1881.

"A Happy Couple," The Cincinnati *Enquirer*, Cincinnati, Ohio, July 27, 1877.

"A Noted Murderer at the Garrison," The Sedalia *Weekly Bazoo*, Sedalia, Missouri, August 23, 1881.

"Abe Rothschild – Motion for a Continuance of His Trial Overruled," The Cincinnati *Enquirer*, Cincinnati, Ohio, May 9, 1878.

"Abe Rothschild – The Questions of His Identity and the Legality of His Arrest," The Cincinnati *Inquirer*, Cincinnati, Ohio Wednesday, March 7, 1877.

"Abe Rothschild Again Betrayed by Glass Eye: Diamond Bessie's Slayer Caught at Get-Rich-Quick Game Here," New York *Tribune*, New York, New York, March 14, 1908.

"Abe Rothschild and his Cell Mate in Irons," The Dallas *Daily Herald*, Dallas, Texas, July 9, 1880.

"Abe Rothschild Convicted of Murder in the First Degree – The Story of the Killing of Diamond Bessie," The Cincinnati *Daily Enquirer*, December 25, 1878.

"Abe Rothschild of Cincinnati," The *Wyandott Herald*, Kansas City, Kansas, December 26, 1878.

"Abe Rothschild to Be Called to an Account on the 7th," The Cincinnati *Enquirer*, Cincinnati, Ohio, May 31, 1880.

"Abe Rothschild, Interviewed by an Enquirer Reporter," The Cincinnati *Enquirer*, Cincinnati, Ohio, December 28, 1878.

"Abe Rothschild," The Cincinnati *Enquirer*, Cincinnati, Ohio, Feb 28, 1877.

"Abe Rothschild: All the Testimony in and Argument of His Case to Begin Today," The Cincinnati Enquirer, Cincinnati, Ohio, December 28, 1880.

"Abe Rothschild: Brought Into Court on a Writ of Habeas Corpus – Arguments Partially Heard, and the Case Still On," The Cincinnati *Enquirer*, Cincinnati, Ohio, August 16, 1877.

"Abe Rothschild: His Arrival in Jefferson, Texas," Cincinnati *Enquirer*, April 17, 1877.

"Abe Rothschild: His Case Called Yesterday, and Postponed Till To-Day," The Cincinnati *Enquirer*, Cincinnati, Ohio, December 18, 1877.

"Abe Rothschild: Opening of the Trial – His Attorneys Fighting the Case at Every Step," The Cincinnati *Enquirer*, Cincinnati, Ohio, December 19, 1877.

"Abe Rothschild: The Sweet Pet of the Texans," The Cincinnati *Enquirer*, Cincinnati, Ohio, April 18, 1877.

"Abe Rothschild: The Testimony as to His Condition," The Cincinnati *Enquirer*, Cincinnati, Ohio, March 4, 1877.

"Abe Rothschild's Case Set for May 7," The Galveston *Daily News*, Galveston, Texas, April 23, 1878.

"Abe Rothschild's Case," The Cincinnati *Enquirer*, Cincinnati, Ohio, October 30, 1880.

"Abe Rothschild's Case," The Cincinnati *Enquirer*, Cincinnati, Ohio, November 20, 1879.

"Abe Rothschild's Case," The Cincinnati *Enquirer*, Cincinnati, Ohio, December 24, 1880.

"Abe Rothschild's Marriage," The Cincinnati *Enquirer*, March 3, 1877.

"Abe Rothschild's Return: Arrival of the Alleged Perpetrator of the Jefferson Woman Murder." Galveston *Daily News*, Galveston, Texas, April 8, 1877.

"Abe Rothschild's Trial," The Galveston *Daily News*, Galveston, Texas, May 25, 1877.

"Abraham Rothschild: The Grand Jury's Opinion," The
    Cincinnati *Enquirer*, Cincinnati, Ohio, May 2, 1877.

"Acquitted," The Chicago *Daily Tribune*, Chicago, Illinois,
    December 31, 1880.

"Affidavit was Made," The Brenham *Weekly Banner*,
    Brenham, Texas, December 9, 1880.

"Amusements," Fort Wayne *Daily Gazette*, Fort Wayne,
    Indiana, April 28, 1881.

"Attempted Escape of Abe Rothschild," The *Times-Picayune*,
    New Orleans, Louisiana, July 12, 1880.

"Backward Glances: Diamond Bessie Murder Case" The Paris
    News, Paris, Texas, April 11, 1941.

"Big Diamond Robbery Played by a Bold Crook on Atlanta
    Merchants," The Atlanta *Constitution*, Atlanta, Georgia
    3/14/1895.

"Bribe Offered to Officers by Abe Rothschild was in
    Counterfeit Money," The Cincinnati *Enquirer*, Cincinnati,
    Ohio, Apr 4 1899.

"Caught In Canada: Coleman, Known as Diamond Charley,
    Arrested and Jailed in Toronto," The Atlanta *Constitution*,
    Atlanta, Georgia 3/25/1895.

"Coleman Has Another Alias," The Atlanta *Constitution*,
    Atlanta, Georgia, March 30, 1895.

"Court of Appeals," The Galveston *Daily News*, Galveston,
    Texas, November 1, 1877.

"Detective Snel," The Cincinnati Enquirer, Cincinnati, Ohio,
    May 5, 1877.

"Diamond Bessie – Strange and Sad History of a Beautiful
    Young Girl," *The National Police Gazette*, May 21, 1878,
    p. 7.

"Diamond Bessie Case One of Most Notorious in Texas
    History," Jefferson *Jimplecute*, June 17, 1965.

"Diamond Bessie Is Marion County's Most Famous Murder
    Case," Jefferson *Daily Jimplecute* April 11, 1937.

"Diamond Bessie's Trunk," The Leavenworth *Times*, Leavenworth, Kansas, August 17, 1880, p. 1. McKay, Mrs. Arch, and Spellings, Mrs. H.A., *A History of Jefferson, Marion County, Texas*. (Jefferson: Christ Episcopal Church).

"Diamond Swindler Guilty," The New York *Times*, New York, NY, September 11, 1902.

"Diamond Swindler is Under Arrest," The Scranton *Republican*, Scranton, PA, June 16, 1902.

"Diamond Thief is Sentenced," The Fort Wayne *News*, Fort Wayne, Indiana, July 20, 1899.

"Doesn't Want To Come Here: Coleman the Diamond Swindler, is Contented in the Canada Jail," The Atlanta *Constitution*, Atlanta, Georgia, March 29, 1895.

"Editorial Notes," Brenham *Weekly Banner*, Brenham, Texas, January 13, 1881.

"Extradited: Abe Rothschild, the Reported Murderer of Bessie Moore, Remanded to the Texas Authorities," The *Daily Milwaukee News*, April 6, 1877.

"For His Life: The Trial of Abe Rothschild," The Cincinnati *Enquirer*, Cincinnati, Ohio, May 25, 1877.

"Four Years for Abe," The Atlanta *Constitution*, Atlanta, Georgia, March 16, 1896.

"Governor Hubbard Proposes," The Austin *Weekly Statesman*, Austin, Texas, May 3, 1877.

"Jefferson Historical Pilgrimage to be Held May 2, 3 and 4," The Mexia *Daily News*, Mexia, Texas, April 25, 1969.

"Local Personals," The Galveston *Daily News*, Galveston, Texas, December 18, 1877.

"Lynch Law" The Chicago *Daily Tribune*, Chicago, Illinois, October 19, 1877.

"Major Abe Rothschild, Once Sentenced to Hang, Risks Contempt," New York *Tribune*, New York, New York, July 28, 1914.

"Mrs. Rothschild's Will Filed," The Cincinnati *Enquirer*, Cincinnati Ohio, January 7, 1915.

"Mysterious Shooting – Was it Assassination or Attempted Suicide?" The Cincinnati *Enquirer*, February 17, 1877.

"Notes by the Way," The Dallas *Daily Herald*, Dallas, Texas, March 4, 1877.

"Off With The Gems" The Atlanta *Constitution*, Atlanta, GA. 3/15/1895.

"Peculiar Practice in Abe Rothschild's Case," The Cincinnati *Enquirer*, Cincinnati, Ohio, November 25, 1880.

"Progress of the Abe Rothschild Murder Case," The Cincinnati *Enquirer*, Cincinnati, Ohio, April 22, 1877.

"Rothschild Will Have a Hard Time," The Cincinnati *Enquirer*, Cincinnati, Ohio, September 20, 1877.

"Southern Gleanings," The Milan *Exchange*, Milan, Tennessee, May 13, 1880.

"Southern States News: Texas," The *Times-Picayune*, New Orleans, Louisiana, June 25, 1878.

"Southern States News: Texas," The *Times-Picayune*, New Orleans, Louisiana, October 21, 1879.

"Squeezing the Squires for Squibs and Squibbles," The Cincinnati *Enquirer*, Cincinnati, Ohio, May 9, 1877.

"State Press," The Galveston *Daily News*, Galveston, Texas, April 26, 1877.

"State Press," The Galveston *Daily News*, Galveston, Texas, January 6, 1881.

"Texas Facts and Fancies," The Austin *Weekly Statesman*, Austin, Texas, January 9, 1879.

"Texas Justice: Abe Rothschild's Escape From a Deserved Hanging," The Cincinnati *Enquirer*, Cincinnati, Ohio, January 25, 1880.

"Texas Murderer Extradited," Oakland *Tribune*, Oakland, California, April 5, 1877.

"Texas," The *Times-Picayune*, New Orleans, Louisiana, November 11, 1877.

"The Acquittal of Abe Rothschild," Fort Wayne *Gazette*, Fort Wayne, Indiana, January 14, 1881.

"The Chain of Evidence Thickens," Fort Wayne *Daily Gazette*, Fort Wayne, Indiana, September 21, 1877.

"The Cincinnati Police Received Award," The Cincinnati *Enquirer*, Cincinnati, Ohio, June 23, 1877.

"The Coffee Was Drugged," The Ogden Utah *Standard*, Ogden, Utah, November 14, 1894.

"The Defense of Abe Rothschild," The *Inter Ocean*, Chicago, Illinois, January1, 1881.

"The Everlasting Rothschild Case," The Austin *Weekly Statesman*, Austin, Texas, January 22, 1880.

"The Judge of the Court Rules in Favor of Abe Rothschild, The Murderer, and Probably Renders His Trial Impossible," The *Times-Picayune*, New Orleans, Louisiana, December 1, 1880.

"The Missing Link: Damning Testimony Against Abe Rothschild – Bessie Moore's Diamonds Found in a St. Louis Pawn Shop," The *Times-Picayune*, New Orleans, Louisiana, September 24, 1877.

"The Murder of Diamond Bessie," *Frontier Times*, Vol. 14, No 8, May 1937.

"The News From Swainsboro," The Atlanta *Constitution*. Atlanta, Georgia, 3/14/1895.

"The Rothschild Case," Brenham *Weekly Banner*, Brenham, Texas, January 16, 1880.

"The Rothschild Case," The *Inter Ocean*, Chicago, Illinois, January 1, 1879.

"The Rothschild Case," The *Times-Picayune*, New Orleans, Louisiana, December 6, 1880.

"The Rothschild Trial: An Interesting Case of Continuance –
Proceedings in Court at Jefferson Yesterday," The
Galveston Daily News, Galveston, Texas, May 26, 1877.

"The Story of the Killing of Diamond Bessie," *The Cincinnati
Daily Enquirer,* December 25, 1878.

"Their Bold Dash: Manacles Bound Two Prisoners Together,
and Together They Escaped," The Fort Wayne *News*. Fort
Wayne Ind., April 7, 1899.

"Trial of Abe Rothschild Begun at Carlisle, Pa.," *The Jewelers'
Circular-Weekly* September 10, 1902.

"Underway – The Trial of Abe Rothschild for Murder," The
Cincinnati *Enquirer*, Cincinnati, Ohio, December 18,
1878.

"Utilizing Abe's Little Adventure as an Advertisement," The
Cincinnati *Enquirer*, Cincinnati, Ohio, January 5, 1881.

Abe Rothschild: His Arrival at Jefferson," The Cincinnati
Enquirer, Cincinnati, Ohio, April 14, 1877.

Bluefield *Daily Telegraph*, Bluefield, West Virginia,
September 17, 1902.

Burger, Michelle, "From Flesh to Bone: The Role of Weather
in Body Decomposition," *Weather.com*, 10/31/2013,
accessed 06/14/2015,
www.weather.com/science/news/flesh-bone-what-role-
weather-plays-body-decomposition-20131031.

Ex Parte Abe Rothschild, Court of Appeals of Texas, 2 Tex.
Ct. App. 560; 1877 Tex. Crim. App. Lexis 188.

Frank, Gustav II. *A Partial List of Earlier Citizens of Jefferson,
Texas, Compiled from Memory*, (Jefferson: Marion County
Genealogical Society, 1960).

Hackney, V.H., *Historical Hallmarks of Harrison County*.
(Marshall, Texas: The Marshall National Bank). 1964.

"Texas," The *Times-Picayune*, New Orleans, Louisiana,
Jan 1 1878.

Harvey, Mary-Margaret. *The History of the Jessie Allen Wise Garden Club, Continued.* (Jefferson: The Jessie Allen Wise Garden Club), 2013.

Letter from Mrs. Riley to Mrs. Jack Ford, President of the Jessie Allen Wise Garden Club, dated February 29, 1956.

McKenzie, Fred. "Historian Locates Bessie Picnic Site," *The Jeffersonian*, Fall/Winter 2003, The Historic Jefferson Foundation.

McKenzie, Fred. *The Abe Rothschild Story.* (Marshall, Texas: The Print Shop), 2003.

Mikkelson, Barbara, "Coined Tradition," *Snopes.com*, 5/18/2014, accessed 4/26/2015, www.snopes.com/military/coins.asp.

Morthland, John. "Cemeteries: The Plots Thicken At Five Final Resting Places That Are Simply To Die For," *Texas Monthly*, March 1999.

Neville, A.W., "Backward Glances: Notables Who Visited Jefferson," The Paris *News*, Paris, Texas, April 2, 1941.

Parmelee, Deolece. *The Deadly Jewels of Diamond Bessie.* Jefferson, Texas: The Jessie Allen Wise Garden Club. 1868.

Raines, Robert K. *Hot Springs: Images of America* (Mount Pleasant, SC: Arcadia Pubishing, 2013).

Russell, Traylor. *Carpetbaggers, Scalawags & Others.* Waco: Texian Press, 1973.

Russell, Traylor. *The Diamond Bessie Murder and the Rothschild Trials.* (Waco, Texas: Texian Press), 1971.

Tarpley, Fred. *Jefferson: Riverport to the Southwest.* (Wolfe City, Texas: Henington Publishing Company), 1983.

The Galveston *Daily News*, Galveston, Texas, Vol. 38, No. 278, February 10, 1880.

The Indianapolis *News*, Indianapolis, Indiana, February 26, 1877.

Venn Dicey, Albert. *Introduction to the Study of the Law of the Constitution*. London: Macmillan And Co., Limited, 1885.

Walters, Mahlon L. "Who Done It to Whom?" Texas Bar Journal, 1963.

Woods, Larry J. "New Speculation about Murder of Diamond Bessie," Jefferson *Jimplecute*, December 11, 1997.

CPSIA information can be obtained
at www.ICGtesting.com
Printed in the USA
FSHW021533101118
53511FS